KILLING THE IMAGE

A CHAMPION'S JOURNEY OF FAITH, FIGHTING, AND FORGIVENESS

ANDRE WARD

WITH NICK CHILES

HARPER
HORIZON

Published by Harper Horizon, an imprint of HarperCollins Focus LLC.

Scripture quotations are taken from the New King James Version®. Copyright
© 1982 by Thomas Nelson. Used by permission. All rights reserved.

Any internet addresses, phone numbers, or company or product information
printed in this book are offered as a resource and are not intended in any way to be
or to imply an endorsement by Harper Horizon, nor does Harper Horizon vouch
for the existence, content, or services of these sites, phone numbers, companies, or
products beyond the life of this book.

ISBN 978-0-7852-9 831-1 (eBook)
ISBN 978-0-7852-9830-4 (HC)

Library of Congress Control Number: 2023940606

Printed in the United States of America
23 24 25 26 27 LBC 5 4 3 2 1

*I want to dedicate this book to my late father, Frank
Ward, and my mother, Madeline Arvie.
Despite everything we have been through, you both
taught me to fight for family and to never give up.
Most importantly, you taught me to acknowledge God
and keep him in his rightful place in my life.
Dad, I am doing the best I can to make you proud every
day. My life is the fruit of your hard work, example, and
sacrifices. I will see you again one day. I love you.
Mom, you have taken an imperfect life and given it to God,
and now he has made your crooked lines straight. You have
more fight in you than anyone I know. You have given me a lot
of that fight too. You are an overcomer, you have persevered,
your life is one of redemption. I am so proud of the mother
and grandmother you are today. Keep going. I love you.*

CONTENTS

CONTENTS

A NOTE ON THE TITLE

My pastor, Napoleon Kaufman, is largely responsible for the title of this book and giving me the push I desperately needed to write the book.

In conversation he said to me, "Dre, you have to 'kill the image.' Who you are is real and the image the world has of you is real, but it's not who you've always been. There are people that need to hear what you've overcome and how you got to where you are today."

He wasn't saying that there was anything pretentious about me, but he was saying that I was free to tell my story. That's just what I did. His words were the seeds that blossomed into the book you now hold in your hands.

PROLOGUE

It's cold and wet outside—I can hear raindrops thudding off of my grandmother's roof one by one as I lie in the dark room. Only a small glimmer of light shines through the torn window curtains. My eyes are fixed on the ceiling; my mouth is dry; my mind is racing. I can hear my heartbeat: *Boom! Boom! Boom!* In the whirlwind of my racing thoughts, my mind slows down long enough for me to catch one—*I'm dying.* I try to take slow, deep breaths and convince myself that I'm okay. My mind tries to control my physical body and command it to do what I need it to do: calm down.

I was eighteen, an elite athlete—this wasn't supposed to be happening to me, but it was. *Should I go get help? Call an ambulance?* I felt trapped between disbelief, shame, and fear. *If I don't call,* I thought, *I might die right here in this room.*

I was scared, but I also knew what had gotten me there, lying on this bed at two a.m. For most of the night, I had been ripping and running with my boys. We were chasing girls, looking for any opportunity to make some money, getting high on weed, drinking alcohol, and popping ecstasy.

Finding ways to escape the pressure and heavy burdens I was shouldering had become my norm. I was hurt, confused, and mad at the world. I needed answers that I felt even God couldn't give me.

I was scared of facing life sober. Alcohol was my counselor. I thought I needed the drugs and alcohol to escape, to numb myself from my daily reality.

But I didn't need this—whatever was happening to me at this moment.

What if I die?

That thought shook me. *What would happen to Tiffiney, the mother of my child? What kind of legacy would I be leaving if I went out like this?* My family would be devastated. One after another, scenes from my life popped into my head, flashing quickly like a movie. That scared me even more.

The pounding in my chest moved up to my eardrums, like my heart was screaming at me. I thought I might be having a drug overdose. At that moment, I realized God had cornered me. I had nowhere else to run, so I did what I was raised to do when I found myself in a tough situation: I looked up and had a conversation with God.

Lord, I know I've been running from you; I know I've messed up. If you let me live, I will never touch another drug and give my life to you. I'm sorry, Lord. Please, please, let me live.

As I lay still, my heart rate began to slow. Before I knew it, I fell asleep. When I woke up a few hours later, I had made it; I was alive. God saw me through. The Olympic gold medal, the world championships, the Hall of Fame almost never happened. But God had his hand on me.

ONE

A CHAMPION IS BORN

I sat on the floor, wide-eyed, as I watched heavyweight champion Michael Moorer hit Big George Foreman at will, round after round, with hard right jabs, straight left hands, and right hooks to the face. Big George kept blinking as he got hit, seemingly unable to evade the blows. But he never stopped coming forward. I was ten years old, sitting close to my dad in front of our big-screen television, one of those heavy old consoles that sat on the floor. I was mesmerized watching these two large men engaged in this sort of poetic, brutal dance with one another. It was the first time I ever paid attention to a live boxing match on TV.

I was a daddy's boy, and my dad, Frank, was heavily invested in the fight. By default, I was heavily invested too. My dad had grown up watching George Foreman, had followed him for a long time. When he settled into his chair to watch Foreman and Moorer go at it, he told me that he had always liked George Foreman because he was mean in the ring and carried a big punch. Big George was also a Christian man and seemed to be a great father. Those were qualities I associated with my dad. So I liked Foreman too.

But things were going badly for Foreman against Moorer. To my eyes, it looked like the younger champion was hitting Big George whenever he wanted, and it didn't seem like there was anything Big George could do about it. This had me and my Dad worried. By the time the fight reached the tenth round, the two commentators said that George might have lost every round. They said it might have been a bad idea that George came back to boxing after a ten-year layoff. He was almost twenty years older than Moorer. The beating was painful to watch. My dad was getting more worried with every round that went by.

But in the tenth round, something happened that shocked me, my dad, and every person in the MGM Grand Garden Arena that night, including Jim Lampley, the lead HBO blow-by-blow commentator.

With 1:18 to go in the round, Big George pushed Moorer back, trying to line him up for a stiff-jab, right-hand, left-hook combo. George parried a right jab from Michael Moorer. Both fighters circled one another. George shot a sharp thudding one-two combo to Moorer's chin. Moorer froze for a split second. George followed up with the same one-two combination. *Boom! Boom!* The two punches landed a half inch closer to the point of Michael Moorer's chin. Time seemed to slow down in that moment. My father and I watched in disbelief as the champion fell straight back, as if someone had pulled a chair out from under him. Michael Moorer was flat on his back. My dad and I looked at each other in shock, then we both leapt to our feet. Moorer slightly lifted his head as if he was going to attempt to get up. Six . . . seven . . . eight . . . Moorer managed to roll over on both knees. Nine . . . ten. The referee waved both hands. The fight was over! Big George did it! We both jumped as high as we could, yelling and screaming. The volume on the TV was blasting.

Lampley belted out, "It happened! It happened!"

"George Foreman has pulled off the miracle no one thought possible!" Gil Clancy, the color commentator, screamed. The cameras cut to Foreman kneeling in a neutral corner, looking up in prayer while people jumped on his back. But Big George didn't flinch; he kept praying.

"Moorer doesn't know where he is! He's still down!" Lampley shouted.

The crowd noise in the arena was deafening. Moorer had been dominating the entire fight up to that fateful moment, but he got careless and he paid for it. Many years later, I would learn this invaluable lesson in my own career, that one punch could change everything. For Michael Moorer that night, it did just that.

The whole spectacle that night did something to me. My father's exuberance, the roar of the crowd in the arena, and specifically the way Jim Lampley captured that moment with genuine excitement and authenticity. He made me feel as though I were right there in the arena. He made the moment come alive for me.

Somewhere in the back of my mind, I logged the whole scene. *What would it feel like to be in that championship ring?* That night, a champion was born. I just didn't know it yet.

My dad, Frank Ward, known as "Duke," was a big dude—six foot two and well over 220 pounds. When he was a high school student in San Bruno, he had taken up boxing as an outlet for his anger and because he liked to fight. Duke was a fast, hard-hitting heavyweight who went 15–0 as an amateur.

He didn't limit his fighting to the ring. My dad was a legendary street fighter in San Bruno. He was fearless, the type of dude you didn't want to see coming at you. He wasn't a bully—in fact, he despised bullies. He was the guy who would always come to the rescue of someone who was being picked on. That's the way he was wired. As kids, my brother and I often got a ringside view of his street-fighting instincts, in addition to his lightning-quick temper. It usually happened when we were out in public and some stranger would stare and give us what my dad used to call "the look."

My father was white and my mother is black. The world saw my brother, Johnathan, and me as two little black boys—in the company of a big white man. For a lot of people, that didn't sit right. They had questions, mostly centered around my father. But my dad didn't play that; he was outraged by the idea of anyone questioning him with his sons. He never started any confrontation, but he certainly would finish it. He was not shy about letting whoever it was feel his outrage.

Often, the fights my dad would get into were with black guys who were misreading the play. They assumed because he was white that there was something soft or weak about him. But their assumptions were painfully off base when it came to Duke Ward. He was not the one you wanted to challenge, especially when it came to his sons.

On many occasions, some dude would look at me and my brother and give Duke the look. Sometimes they would mumble under their breath, "What's he doing with those black boys?"

I would feel my anxiety start to rise and I would get a knot in my stomach. I knew things were about to get spunky.

"Wait, what'd you say?" my dad would ask, whipping his head around.

His muscle memory from the years in the ring and in the streets would instantly be activated. I saw my father punch guys in the face quicker than I could even cover my eyes. Duke had hands.

It got to the point where I didn't want to go with my dad to the store because I was afraid of what might happen. Don't get the wrong idea: my dad was a gentle giant. His normal demeanor was to mind his own business, go to work, and take care of his boys. But if you looked at any of us the wrong way, you can be sure you were gonna get a reaction.

The conflicts were terrifying, but I can't say that I completely disliked them. There was a part of me that was proud of my dad for the way he stood up and protected our family.

"Son, people are looking at you because I'm white," he'd say to me as an explanation. "But they shouldn't be doing that. That's not right. It doesn't matter what skin color we have. You're my son. I love you."

My dad always made sure that my brother and I knew that he loved us. He was very open and honest with his feelings and showed us a lot of affection, something he always told me that he didn't receive as a child. My dad was doing everything in his power to make sure that me and my brother were not going to have the same testimony. The way my father loved us would ultimately break generational curses in our family. The Ward men who came before him had no problem showing affection to the women in the family but displayed toxic masculinity toward one another. My father was sowing the seeds that would ultimately produce better fruit in my life as I became a man. By his example, my father gave me the license to be a strong man, a protector, but also one who knew how to love, not just in word but in deed.

It was my father's love of the sport that led me to boxing. I deeply valued the stories he told me about his boxing career at Crestmoor High School. I could not believe they had a boxing team at his school.

"They let you box in high school?" I asked, amazed. The 1970s sounded like a wild place. The man I loved and admired more than anybody in the world got in the ring and knocked people out? I was in.

"You boxed. I want to box," I told him.

5

He eyed me closely. He wouldn't be Frank Ward if he didn't see an opportunity here to deliver a message. "Listen. Boxing is not a game," he said. "If we do this, you have to stick with it."

That's the day we went down to a local gym in Hayward called U.S. Karate and Boxing. It's in a nondescript little building on Industrial Parkway, a major commercial strip in Hayward. We tried to get to the gym before it closed, but when we got there the lights were out and the door was locked. My dad could see the disappointment on my face; I could never hide my emotions. My dad walked off and motioned for me to follow him. He was standing underneath a large broken window on the side of the building. He told me to get on his shoulders and he lifted me up so I could see inside through the cracked window. Sitting in the middle of the floor of the gym was a boxing ring. It was the first time I had ever laid eyes on a real ring. It was grimy, but I was awestruck. I was only ten, but I knew I was seeing something special. Before I had even set foot inside the place, I was already starting to fall in love.

TWO

GENERATIONAL CURSES AND BLESSINGS

My childhood featured so much movement and disruption that my memories of my dad and my mom being together are hazy. My timeline of those years jumps around, from one vivid scene to another, but with no month or year to match them with. What I do remember is how my mom and dad interacted with each other on any given day. I was always hypersensitive to their movements toward one another. *Are they getting along? Does Dad look upset? Oh, they seem happy right now.* Those were my cues to tell me how the day was going to go.

My mother, Madeline Arvie, was born in San Francisco in 1960, the middle child of three kids. Her childhood was stable, middle class, with her mother and father in the home, and her mother intent on filling the lives of her children with vacations, plays, movies, short trips—as many cultural experiences as she could find. They sampled a wide range of cuisines, went out of the country a few times to places like Vancouver, and made their share of treks to Disneyland. My grandparents' roots were embedded in the South—my grandmother, Lorene Dimmer Arvie, was from Arkansas, and my grandfather, Isaac Arvie Sr., was from Louisiana.

From the outside, it appeared that my mother was living a fairy tale. But that image would come to haunt her when she reached middle school. When kids saw somebody living a life they'd never had, one they longed for, their response was harsh. My mother became the target of jealous middle-school bullies. Kids would push her, hit her, try to make her start fighting. At first, she would back off and try to get away.

"You better start hitting those kids back because that's the only way they're going to stop," her mother would tell her.

It wasn't long before my mom discovered that she could fight.

"I beat the brakes off of them," she would tell me. "Good enough for them to stop bullying me."

My mother made it clear that my own fighting ability comes from her just as much as my dad.

When my mother was in high school, she met a boy she liked; he became her first serious boyfriend. That relationship led to a teenage pregnancy. When she was seventeen, just after graduating from high school, she gave birth to her first child—my sister Jasmine. Ten and a half months later, my sister Tasha was born. When things didn't work out with their father, my mother moved in with my grandmother—who was affectionately known to our family as Mommo.

When her father, who owned a construction company, started working a job out in Ocean Beach in San Francisco, my mother would occasionally tag along. One day she met some girls around her age and started hanging with them. It wasn't long before these girls had pulled my mother down into a world of heavy drug use. They would mix cocaine with ether and smoke the white shavings that bubbled up to the top of the bottle. She would take a few hits and feel good; that's all she felt she needed. But eventually, these girls graduated to smoking crack, like many were doing during this period in the 1980s. My mom found herself meeting up with these girls so often that she began to let everything else slip. Within a year, she had a full-blown addiction.

My sisters stayed with Mommo, who insisted that she would watch the kids until Mom got herself together. My mother knew her kids were feeling neglected, but she didn't have enough strength and control of herself to change the picture. This is the danger with substance abuse. By the time you realize you have a problem that you can't control, it's too late. She would get jobs at various construction sites to keep enough money coming in that she could satisfy her needs.

When my mother was twenty-one, living in the Westlake Village apartments in San Francisco, she met a good-looking white guy who was working maintenance there. That was Frank Ward, my dad. Within a short period of time, they fell in love. They had something special between them, a strong connection that would be tested constantly in the coming years. At this point, neither of them was aware of the other's substance abuse issues, but that would soon change.

After high school, my dad had moved into a house with two guys, one of whom was a serious drug user. In the 1970s, the area was flooded with cheap heroin; he and his friends quickly began to lose themselves in the culture. At first, they would use heroin sporadically, maybe one Friday a month. Then it became every other week; soon it was several times a week. My dad's close friend, who I call Uncle Bob, told me that my father showed up to his place one night with a brand-new Triumph motorcycle.

"Bobby, I need you to take this bike," Duke said.

"What? Did you run over somebody? What's going on?"

"No, no, I don't want the bike. I want you to just keep it here. If I come back and say I need it, don't give it to me."

My father later told Uncle Bob he was afraid he would sell the bike for drugs. That's how bad it had gotten for him. Uncle Bob noticed that his friend was sometimes zoned out, but my father said it was just marijuana. Uncle Bob believed him because my dad was functioning, still able to hold down jobs and be out in the world. But that lifestyle wasn't sustainable for him. Uncle Bob always felt like the drugs stopped my father from making it in the sport of boxing. He had a front-row seat to my father's amateur career, had sparred with him on many occasions; he knew my father was special. He felt the addiction robbed him of so much of what he could have been.

When Duke began a relationship with my mother in the early eighties, she didn't notice anything that hinted at a drug problem—at least at first. She did find it odd that when she would spend the night with him, he would get up every morning and leave the apartment. She was a little suspicious of where he was going, but he always brought back coffee and donuts as a way to explain his early morning departures. But there were other things that didn't make sense to her.

"He would be nodding off. Sometimes he would just go to sleep," she said. "At first, I just thought that meant he was tired because he was working all the time. It never dawned on me that it was drugs. So finally I asked him about it. And he told me what was going on, that he had been using prior to us becoming a couple. That was heavy for me to hear. I had to face his demons as well as my own."

When he was waking up in the morning, he was going to a clinic to get methadone. He told her he had been battling addiction for several years, but he felt that he was getting it under control. Most addicts feel this way. The two of them were like matching bookends, hoping their love was strong enough to overcome the monsters that had ahold of their minds and bodies.

A couple years into their relationship, my mother started feeling familiar things happening inside her body. When she went to the doctor, she was told that she was two months pregnant, and she had to have an uncomfortable conversation with the doctor, letting him know that she had been using drugs. Ultimately, she chose to stop using drugs until after I was born.

My mother told me that it had been hard for her to stop at other times, but when she found out she was pregnant with me, she just stopped using. She knew it was God keeping her clean and that I was going to be a special child.

God had his hand on me and had a plan for my life before I was even born.

In those early years, the thing that felt most constant to me was movement, unpredictability, bouncing around to the households of different family members, living in lots of places, even hotels at certain stints. My parents were in love, but that wasn't enough. They had their winning seasons together, but they just couldn't do right long enough to make it a consistent thing.

When I was three years old, my father got admitted to a drug treatment facility in Berkeley called New Bridge Foundation, a well-known program around the corner from the Cal Berkeley campus. My mother brought me and my brother, Johnathan, to visit him. Johnathan is my father's son from a previous relationship. We had no idea what he was doing at this place. I just remember that the program was strict, with a lot of rules. Once he completed the program, he came back home to us.

Unfortunately, sometime in the next year or so, my mother relapsed and started using again. This would be a recurring theme throughout the years. She became a shadowy presence, here for a week, gone for six or seven months at a time, and sometimes longer. I could tell her absence was eating away at my dad, and it wasn't until many years later that I would realize that her absence was having a profound negative effect on me. There always seemed to be a cloud of tension whenever my mother did show up from one of her stints in the streets. I wasn't old enough to know exactly what was going on, but I often had an unsettled feeling in my gut, always bracing for the next explosive blowup between them. I didn't know what or who was going to start it, I didn't know how it would end, but I did know it was going to be bad. Even when there was a slice of relative peace in the house, I could never really enjoy it because I was bracing for the next fight. The fights would inevitably start when my mother would ask for money because she was ready to leave and head back to San Francisco, her stomping grounds—the place she was when she wasn't with me.

We spent a lot of time with Mommo in Daly City. She was trying to make sure we were being cared for throughout all the chaos in our house. Wherever I was, I spent long stretches looking out the window, waiting for my mom to show up. It was an ache that I carried around with me, wondering where she was and why she had left me again. But no matter who I was living with at the time, I always felt the love of those around me.

I'm not sure what the custody arrangement was, but my father would pick me up from Mommo's house on the weekends and take me to his house in the East Bay. On this particular weekend, the cops showed up. As I peeked outside the window, I saw my father talking to them. Apparently he hadn't brought me back to Mommo's house when he was supposed to. I was the baby in the family and was always taken care of, but I wanted to live with my father. Mommo called the cops; they showed up to take me back. I heard bits and pieces of what they were saying. He told them that I was his son and he should have the right to keep me because my mother wasn't around and I wanted to stay with him. They must have taken his side in the dispute because I didn't go back to live with Mommo from that day forward.

When Mom did show up, I would be very happy to see her. All would be forgiven. I didn't know or care about what was keeping her away, I just wanted her home with me. As a young boy I could tell that she didn't look right at times. Things would just feel off. Even at a young age I had good instincts and was very observant. It wasn't like Mom showed up high, but her hair would be messy, her clothes disheveled. She had the appearance of someone who was surviving on the streets. I'd hear people in the family whispering about her, how she struggled with addiction and the effects it was having on me. My dad would always defend my mother to anyone he heard talking about her.

I didn't fully understand it, but I did know she seemed to always be gone or about to leave. *When is she leaving?* That question was always there, bouncing around my head. It got worse and worse.

Each night, I would get on my knees and pray: *God, please bring my mom home. Please don't let her die out there in the streets.*

Sometimes she would call and say she was coming to visit. I'd get excited—but she wouldn't always show up. That made my father angry. I'm sure the bitterness, resentment, and unforgiveness he carried toward my mother at that time must have been immeasurable. He genuinely loved my mother and wanted to be with her. At that time, my mother was married to the streets and her addiction wouldn't allow her to love him back the same way. More than anything, he wanted her to be there for me, but that just was not our reality. My dad was struggling to raise two boys as a single father, and I know he could have used some help. I will never forget how much Dad watched over and cared for me and my brother during those stretches. We needed him. He had his own struggles, but that's the type of man he was. I don't know where

I would be if I didn't have those years with him—I certainly wouldn't be the man I am today. His attitude was, "If I'm going to struggle, I'm going to struggle with you—I'm not leaving my boys." He had a great deal of integrity.

One altercation between my parents is still branded in my brain. Mom was ready to leave; she was rested, fed, and had spent a few days with me. She asked Dad for money, but he pushed back because he knew what the money was for. My father was still struggling with his own demons of addiction; he understood the tendencies of someone with that mindset.

"I know why you want money, and I'm not giving it to you," he said.

Things quickly turned physical. I was waiting for Dad to bring me to my baseball game. I was about nine. It was an all-star game and I was going to be the starting pitcher, so I was anxious to leave. I was sitting downstairs waiting when I heard an eruption upstairs. The two of them came out of my father's room yelling at each other, and my mother was taking swings at my father while she was yelling. They kept fighting all the way down the stairs. As I watched in shock, I saw that there were long, bright-red streaks of blood on the wall. My mother had stabbed my father in his side.

I didn't know if the police were going to come or if my dad was going to die, but his injury wasn't life-threatening; he didn't even go to the hospital. The two of them cleaned the blood off the walls and my mother left. Dad got things together enough to bring me to my game, but I was still in shock when we arrived. I was a really good baseball player, an outstanding pitcher and shortstop. For the first couple of innings, I couldn't get the sight of the blood out of my mind. I was literally shaking as I stood there on the mound, peering into the catcher's mitt. I walked a few batters and gave up a few hits. I knew something was off, but by the third inning I had settled down. This was probably the first appearance of a trait that every elite athlete must learn: how to compartmentalize. Years later this trait would become one of my strongest assets as a fighter—the ability to, while under immense pressure, remain focused and execute a game plan. That day on the pitcher's mound, I learned the importance of focus. I started to learn how to bury things—pain, discomforting thoughts, unsettling emotions. That became my defense mechanism to deal with all the adverse childhood experiences I endured.

I don't share these stories to express any lingering bitterness toward my mom or my dad. By the grace of God and much counsel, I've been set free from that. I refuse to point fingers at either of them or blame them for the things that I experienced in my life. Through my personal walk with Jesus Christ, I've gotten the revelation that I, too, needed to be forgiven. If I was unwilling to forgive, how could I seek forgiveness from God or anyone else?

My parents did the best they could with what they had. They grew up in an era when access to drugs was exploding around the nation while ignorance about the effects of drugs remained high—creating a perfect storm. When my mother began experimenting with drugs, her intent was to have a good time and escape the pressures of life. She had no idea that this was the start of a lifelong battle that would take a toll on her mind, her body, and her family. By the time she realized she had a problem, it was far too late.

Despite all the stresses I experienced because of my parents battling addiction, I was generally a happy kid: quiet but watchful, learning and always processing. The adults around me observed how I was "always watching everybody." They told me I had an "old soul," interested in grown folks' business, asking questions that most little boys would never think to ask at that age. Still, I was also known for my big, bright smile, a sign that life's circumstances hadn't broken me. I was a normal kid who had real life issues going on around him that he didn't fully understand. I felt the burden of wanting my mom to be around, yet I was always surrounded by love from family on both sides—black and white. The love I received shielded me from the reality of my situation. My family also did all they could to protect me. I'd hear a lot of "Your mom, she's gonna be alright" or "Your mom is in San Francisco, but you'll see her soon."

We weren't rich by any stretch of the imagination. We had our struggles like many families do, but I was always taken care of. It was my uncle Isaac buying me shoes and clothes; it was Mommo taking care of me. If it wasn't Mommo, it was ReRe, my mother's sister. If it wasn't ReRe, it was my dad. Or my other aunts—my dad's sisters—Sandy, Sue, and Boopsie. I was never without. The only thing I was lacking was the family structure that I wanted. But in the midst of that, the love was real. The love from my father was real. The love from my mother was real. They both were just battling something for which they were no match.

THREE

BEAUTIFUL STRUGGLE

When I first walked into U.S. Karate and Boxing, I was instantly intoxicated by the smell, the sounds, the feel of the place. I had never been in a boxing gym before. The ring dominated the room. You could hear the rhythmic sound of fighters hitting the heavy bags, mitts, and speed bags. After my dad signed me up, the owner of the gym, a man named Joe Silva, placed me with the head trainer of the gym, a small Hispanic man named Seraphine. My dad had a conversation with the trainer about his training philosophy. I didn't hear everything they said, but the takeaway from Seraphine was, *I'm gonna make him tough. I'm gonna get him in shape. He may have to take two punches to land one, but we're gonna wear his opponents down.*

My dad wasn't crazy about what he had heard from Seraphine. He didn't appreciate that philosophy when it came to his son. We tried Seraphine out for a little while. After a week or so, we noticed another guy in the gym, a tall, light-skinned black man who was also a trainer. I saw my dad talking to him, but I didn't know what was going on.

When I was hitting the heavy bag, I would periodically stop to look over at him. He was nodding at me real slow, as if he were saying, *Hey, I see you.*

After my training that day, my dad told me that the guy's name was Virgil Hunter. "I kind of like his style, Dre," my dad said, "because I don't want you taking any unnecessary punishment. I want you to learn how to hit and not get hit."

My dad was a big fan of Muhammad Ali; he even copied Ali's style when he boxed, moving lightly on his toes. Ali didn't believe in taking unnecessary punches either.

That was the first time I ever heard of that concept: hit and not get hit. The idea of fighting with a main goal of minimizing the blows you take, versus fighting solely to demonstrate your toughness, represented a dichotomy that has existed in boxing for a very long time. Boxing writers and fans will praise a fighter who stands there and takes a lot of punishment, calling them tough, intoxicated by their grit and resiliency. Virg was taught by a generation of trainers who came from an era when boxers, particularly black boxers, in order to eat, had to take underground fights, fights on a week's notice, fights in backwoods and other places where the ref might not be able to save you. You had to know how to fight and defend yourself, how to be smart in the ring, or you weren't going to survive. This style of fighting is not a novel concept. In fact, it has been around for a very long time, especially among black trainers. Trainers like Virg saw their sole purpose as getting you home safe to your family.

After a couple of weeks, Virgil came to our house to do a test run with me to see if we were a good fit. We did it away from the gym and Seraphine to conceal that Virg was potentially poaching me away. We went out onto the back deck, which was shaped like a boxing ring. Right away, the training felt different. Virg had these big black training mitts;

he held them up and moved around, telling me to hit the target. He had a rhythm to how he worked, how he moved. It was like an orchestrated dance. We did drills for about half an hour. When we were done, I had a big smile on my face. I had a lot of fun with Virg that day.

The first time Virg slid the gloves on my hands to spar against an opponent in the ring, admittedly I was scared. I had been training with him for a few weeks when he decided it was time to see what I looked like under fire. My opponent was a Filipino kid named Glenn Donaire. Glenn and his brother, Nonito, both trained at the gym. Glenn is four years older than me, but we were about the same size at the time. There's a big difference between a nine-year-old and a fourteen-year-old in physical strength, even if they are a similar size. Not only was Glenn stronger, he also hit extremely hard. He didn't know how to go easy on the new kid. The first time, I was moving, dancing, running for my life. I grabbed him and held on, trying to avoid getting hit. But I still got hit with a couple of shots. My heart was racing; my mind wasn't far behind; I'd never been in a situation like this before. But Virg was coaching me through the whole thing.

"You're good . . . Calm down . . . Get yourself together . . . Give yourself some space."

After a couple of rounds, Virg abruptly stopped the sparring session. "That's good. That's all we need. I wanted to see where he's at."

Glenn was trained by Seraphine, so every time we got in the ring there was probably a little desire to get back at Virg for convincing me to train with him. When Virg called it, my dad and Virg were standing together in my corner. I could hear their conversation.

"He ain't got it," my dad said about me, looking at Virg. "He ain't got it."

"Hold on now, Duke," Virg responded. "Give him a little time."

I could see my dad's face. Clearly, he was disappointed. He said that boxing might not be the right sport for me. I didn't know what to believe. *Was Virg right or was my father right?* But it wasn't in my nature to give up. I knew I couldn't quit.

It was such a God thing for me to have Virg there to balance out my dad. Duke was always an all-or-nothing kind of guy, which is why he couldn't train me. When things went wrong, or I wasn't doing something right, he'd get frustrated, angry: "I told you to get your hands up!" followed by a few expletives. I would just shut down.

Right in front of me I saw what would happen if Virg wasn't around, because my father decided to train my brother, Johnathan. Johnathan had been watching all the excitement brewing in the house because of my interest in boxing and how it was grabbing so much of our father's attention, so he said he wanted to box too. Dad had the idea that Virg would train me and he would train Johnathan. My brother probably thought it was gonna be cool, but it didn't turn out that way at all. I would be having fun in the gym with Virg and then I'd look over at my brother and I'd feel sorry for him. My dad would be grilling him, putting him through it. "I told you to use your *bleep-bleep* jab a thousand times," I would overhear from my dad. It didn't look like fun at all. But instead of saying he wanted to train with Virgil, Johnathan didn't speak up. We didn't have our mothers around, so our dad was all we had. We never wanted to do anything to disappoint him.

Virgil was in my ear constantly, telling me I was getting better, filling me with his long-term vision that helped me believe that I could do it.

"You keep doing these drills? Watch—you're going to be sharp, Dre! You just got started. You gotta remember, Dre, he's like fourteen years old. In six months, you'll be dominating him."

He was always reminding me of the context of the situation, painting a picture so I could catch the vision. I kept working the heavy bag, kept working on the drills. Having fun while learning and growing as a fighter. A few weeks later, I was back in the ring with Glenn.

The next time we went a little bit longer, four rounds. I was starting to hold my own. My confidence, my comfort, just grew, little by little. After a while, I started to believe. *I can do this.*

Virg was a master of using descriptive words; he enabled me to see things by explaining difficult concepts in their simplest form. And he was always so sure, so confident, that I absorbed his confidence. He'd say, "You do this for a month, you're going to start to see." And then I would see it. That would reaffirm to me: this guy knows what he's talking about.

I learned a powerful lesson in those early months: "Death and life are in the power of the tongue" (Proverbs 18:21). If you berate your son or daughter day in and day out, you're going to eat the fruit of what you are saying to them. You're going to see that thing mature and become a self-fulfilling prophecy. Especially for the young, be mindful of what you say to them, what's being poured into them. And we also need to be mindful of what we are telling ourselves, because people become what they think. I was able to take these things that Virg was saying to me and internalize them, believe them, and put them into action. When I was in the very beginning stage of boxing, by all accounts the optics didn't look good. It didn't look like I had it. But I just needed time, nurturing, development, patience. Virg gave me all those things, as did my dad—just not in a trainer role. I had all the goods; I just needed somebody who could recognize that and help me bring it all out.

It was important to Virg and to my dad that I be battle hardened in that gym before I had my first amateur fight. Some guys go out there right away, looking for a fight after two or three months in the gym.

But my people didn't believe in that. After a few months, I heard my father say, "He's looking good, Virg. He's looking good." I was now holding my own against Glenn. We were looking much more evenly matched. Virg would frequently be in my father's ear: "Duke, did you see that? Look at Dre—you see that? He put together a three-punch combination right there!"

Hearing Virgil's voice and confidence was pivotal for my dad. He didn't want me to get hurt, so he was overprotective of me. After a few more months, they decided it was time for me to hit the road, to get outside of our home gym and find other guys to spar. We called it gunslinging.

Virg would be on the phone: "You got a kid? How much does he weigh? Okay, Dre's walking around at about ninety-five pounds right now. Your kid is one hundred pounds? Well, how old is he? How many fights does he have? Okay, we'll come up there for some work."

The first time I walked into King's Boxing Gym in Oakland at about ten years old, everything felt and looked different, but I heard the same familiar, rhythmic sounds: the jump ropes, the speed bags, the heavy bags, the sparring in the ring, the coaches yelling instructions. The best gyms are beautiful scenes of controlled chaos. They had high-level boxers training in there—*This guy is a contender, that guy is about to fight for the state championship, that guy might be heading to the Olympics.* My ten-year-old mind was blown. I had never seen anything like it. I was excited—and a little intimidated. This was a new gym, new territory, and a bunch of new faces.

At U.S. Karate and Boxing, the ring wasn't much higher than the floor. But the ring at King's looked professional—you had to walk up these big steps to reach it. When guys were sparring, everybody crowded around the ring to watch—and comment, like a real fight. The first two guys I sparred with were named Alex and Ray. Everybody called Ray "Sweet N Low." They were both trained by Wesley, a well-known trainer in the area.

Sparring isn't an actual bout; a winner is not declared. A fighter is supposed to be working on different parts of their game, but Virgil was teaching me to dominate and not just hold my own, to have everyone talking about me when I finished. The reality is sparring is a lot about bragging rights. When you step out of the ring, you want people to say, "Hey man, you did your thing today." I wasn't one of those fighters who loved sparring. I'd always get knots in the pit of my stomach because I put so much pressure on myself. I always wanted to do good, to look good. I didn't want to have a bad day. That feeling continued throughout my professional career.

A crowd had gathered for my first session at King's Gym because I was the visiting fighter. This was probably the biggest audience I'd had up to that point. When the sparring session was over, the older fighters and trainer immediately had words for me.

"Good work, youngster!"

"Hey man, you a bad boy!"

"Good work in there!"

A few directed their comments to Virg, who was known throughout the Oakland boxing community. "Ay, Virg, you got a bad boy right there!"

I received a lot of praise that day; I felt like I was on top of the world. I walked in there nervous; now I was walking out with my head held high. I got nods of approval from Virg and from my dad. I gained respect in a new gym. It was a big day for me. I walked out of the gym that day with the thought in my head, *Yeah, I can definitely do this.*

At that point I knew there was no turning back. I had a coach. Money was being spent and credit cards were being maxed out for gas, hotel rooms, and equipment. I had to push the other sports to the side.

Boxing is a jealous sport. It's not seasonal; I learned that it requires maximum effort if you want to be the best. If you dedicate yourself to it, the sport can reward you in your biggest moments. But if you cheat, if you slack and don't respect it, it will expose you when you least need it. Boxing was my life now.

My mother wasn't around much in these years, but my dad was doing well with his business, Mobile Glass. He carted the glass around in a big, red, rusty Chevy truck. I *hated* that truck. When he'd try to drop me off at school, I'd ask him to let me out a block away. If he was picking me up, he'd pull up in the ugly truck, with the exhaust rumbling and popping, looking like he had stolen Fred Sanford's truck from *Sanford and Son*. He didn't understand my disdain.

My dad was working a lot at the time, but when he came home, we would chill for a while, talking about our day. After a while, he would routinely go up to his room and disappear. I would always hear the water running in his bathroom. When he would come out of his room, an hour or so later, he'd be a different person. His face would be red; he didn't look right. He'd be groggy, nodding off, going in and out. He'd tell us to do off-base things, like do some chores around the house at eight o'clock at night, but he could barely keep his eyes open. Sometimes he would make a sandwich—he loved peanut butter and jelly—and would nod off right in the middle of eating it. I would look at him closely, asking myself, *What is wrong with him?* I couldn't figure it out. I knew he wasn't drunk because he often said he would never touch alcohol after growing up with an alcoholic dad. He was a single dad who owned a business, so I knew he was working hard every day. And carrying and installing heavy sheets of glass was backbreaking work. *That must be it, he's just tired from work, or maybe he took some sleeping pills or something.* But deep down, I knew that wasn't enough of an explanation. Why did he stay in his room so long with the door closed? Why did he run the water so long? What was the water for, maybe to drown out some type of noise? I was confused.

This had been going on for some time until the day I was looking around for something in my dad's room and came across an object wrapped in cloth, lying on the floor next to his bed. I found two needles and immediately dropped them. I froze. I was confused, so I called my dad and told him what I had found.

"Oh yeah, I found those outside," he told me. "I wanted to bring them inside so nobody picked them up. Just leave them alone. Don't touch them, okay?" That explanation didn't sound right, but what was I supposed to do, tell him I thought he was lying?

He had always complained about pain in his back and sometimes he took pills to fight the pain. My dad had shared that he had a history with drugs. But at that age, I really couldn't quantify how bad his previous drug problem really was. And I didn't know enough about drugs to know that needles were involved.

I did as I was told and tried to put the incident out of my mind, but it's something that's always stayed with me. Many more months went by. Dad continued to show up groggy, continued to nod off. One day he came to us and said, very somberly, "I need to talk to you guys."

My brother and I eyed each other, wondering what was going on. We didn't have any other siblings in the house; it had always been just the two of us. Every struggle we went through, every high we went through, every trauma we went through, we got through it together. We assessed every situation together, trying to figure out what it meant.

He sat us down, his face full of shame. He told us that he had started using drugs again.

"What? What do you mean?" I asked.

"I started using again, and I gotta go into a program," he said. "I'm doing this for you guys. I can't keep living like this. I have to check myself in."

I had heard he had been in a program in his younger years, so I knew that was a thing. But hearing Superman tap out and say, "Man, I can't do it anymore"—that didn't feel right.

He continued. "Millie and Virg—you guys are going to live with them."

He told us Virg and his wife Millie had agreed to take us in while he got better. As he talked, I was trying to put the pieces together. My life had seen its share of disruption and chaos. We were finally in a good, stable place—now *this*?

Packing up the house was hard. We had had good times in that house. We knew it was the last time we would ever sleep in our rooms, ever sit together at the kitchen table. I knew my father was going to have some rough days ahead in rehab. This wasn't going to be some short thirty-day stay in Victory Outreach rehab program. He was trying to beat heroin for good. It was going to be a long, painful battle.

I never really said goodbye to my friends on Kelly Hill, the neighborhood I lived in at that time. I had a lot of close friends who lived in that neighborhood. I didn't even know what I would say—*Um, yeah, my dad is going to a drug rehab program so we gotta move*. Nah. I was an '80s baby, and I was raised to never share your family's personal business with anyone outside your home. I never liked goodbyes anyway. It was better to just cut ties and keep it moving.

My brother and I had been going back and forth to Millie and Virg's house for a while; my father would drop us off there for a few days, a weekend here and there, maybe to give himself some space. Johnathan and I were very comfortable with them by this time. But now both of my parents would be out of my life? What was that going to feel like?

What I didn't know was that this was the last time me and my father would ever live in the same house together.

Our arrival at Virg and Millie's home came at an interesting time for Virg, who had now become my godfather. Like all trainers, he always had his eyes peeled for the next champion he could take under his wings. He worked in the Alameda County Probation Department and had a special touch and a gift with young men. He knew how to reach them, get them to open up, and he was also a good listener. Years earlier he had trained a kid named Bosco who looked really promising. But Virg lost him to the streets; he wound up being sent to a California Youth Authority (now the California Division of Juvenile Justice) facility and it was a wrap. That was a common theme—he'd get these guys cleaned up and on the road to a boxing career, then the streets would push Virg out of the way and devour them. He'd even trained his own son, Jovan, who had a lot of promise. But then Jovan's mother snatched him out of Virgil's life. I think Virg was in the middle of mourning Jovan when I came into his life. He always said I was a godsend to him.

Because we had spent so much time with Virgil and Millie already, we were accustomed to how they did things, the rhythms of their household. They lived in a townhouse with three floors. Johnathan slept in the small room off the garage on the first floor; my room was on the second floor, across the hall from Virg and Millie's room. On the top floor was the living room, kitchen, and dining room area. It was nice, and it felt like a safe place for us. I didn't feel like the police were going to be banging on the door or something crazy might jump off at any moment. At my dad's, while he always kept us safe, there was an instability in the house that I now recognize as the drugs at work. The security and stability were the things I most loved about staying with Virg and Millie.

The house was in a calm, middle-class neighborhood. The gym

was right down the street. While Virg was more about fun, Millie was the strict disciplinarian. She would stay on top of us about our school-work and chores. She was heavy-handed with it, which is what we needed, but that would sometimes lead to conflict. It was hard taking orders from a woman who was not my mother, and I was vocal about it.

"You're not my mom!" I said to Millie on more than one occasion— something I'm not proud of. I looked at everything through the filter of my mother not being there. However, my brother and I did love and appreciate Millie a lot. Virg would put a lot on her plate when it came to us. Millie would always deliver, always have food on the table to keep our bellies full. We loved her for all of that. This was a woman who didn't have any children, who was accepting two preteen boys in her house and becoming a mother figure overnight. I recognize now that she was trying to figure it all out, just as we were. I was raised to respect authority and respect my elders, but we had our disagreements. I'm not stupid—I wasn't the type to yell and scream at an adult. But I might say something fresh under my breath. "Man, I can't stand this." That sort of thing.

It was a bit rocky at first. But eventually we found our rhythm, our own way of being together. And in the back of my mind, I knew that I didn't have anywhere else to go. My mother was still working through her issues. She was clean and doing better, but she still wasn't in a place where I could live with her. So I always had a great deal of gratitude toward Millie. I knew Virg and Millie were godsent to fill a void that desperately needed filling and to give me and big bro some much-needed stability.

I think Virg and Millie treated me and Johnathan as equally as possible, but with two very different kids, that's not always going to look the same. I was probably a little closer to Virg because I loved boxing so much. I watched boxing constantly, I asked questions about boxing, I'd be knocking on Virg's door, asking, "When are we going to the gym?" My brother was more to himself. He did the boxing thing because he accepted that we were a boxing family, but he didn't love it the way I did. I don't know if it was true at the time, but beneath the surface Johnathan and I kind of felt that our staying there was a bit transactional in nature. You're my trainer, we moved in with y'all, so we need to keep boxing. Johnathan was initially trying to please Dad with the boxing; now he was trying to please Virgil. But while I was watching boxing matches, studying everything about Roy Jones Jr.— even trying to copy his hairstyle and the way he dressed—Johnathan was downstairs watching cartoons.

We would get the chance to visit my dad at the program some-times. Those occasions were bittersweet—happy to see him, happy that he looked like he was doing good, but also in pain because we couldn't be together. It felt like he was in prison. We consistently exchanged letters back and forth, enough for me to fill up an old suitcase with. He would ask how things were going with Millie and Virg, ask about an upcoming tournament, encourage us to keep training hard. After he got out of the program, he would visit us. On occasion he would spend the night. But as much as my dad wanted to be with us, he wasn't one to be living on another man's couch, so the overnights didn't happen much. More often he would stay for a few hours and then take off. It was clear he wanted to be around us as much as he could. He was bouncing around a lot, staying with his sister Sandy or in a motel. He didn't have much stability at that time. I always felt like he would come back and get us. That was the hope I held onto. But it never happened.

Going through adolescence in somebody else's house wasn't easy. That stuff is hard enough when you're under your parents' roof—living with two people who aren't your parents was extremely hard. I was trying to figure out a lot of it on my own. I just didn't feel comfortable talking about it. My brother and I would discuss things, but he was just as ignorant about what was happening as I was. Virg knew how to talk to young men, how to pull things out of them, but I don't remember having any meaningful conversations about sex. Sometimes he would tease me about it. "Yeah, I see you looking at that girl," he said more than once. But I was never going to come to him with all the questions spinning around in my head.

When I started high school, I was a clean-cut kid with a reputation as a rising boxer. Girls liked me, but I was a little square. Boxing took up so much of my time that I didn't have the space to hang out and go to parties. I got all As my freshman year. My schedule was simple: school, home, gym, home, eat, homework, bed. Not much deviation at all.

I got it in my head my freshman year that I wanted to play football. But there was just one problem: my dad refused to let me play. I thought it was crazy that he would let me box but not let me play football.

"You could break your neck," he said more than once. "It's dangerous."

I was getting burned out with boxing; football looked like a lot of fun. So I snuck on the team anyway. Virg started to get suspicious when I'd come home from school all sweaty with dirt under my fingernails. But he didn't say anything to me about it. Virg is a master chess player.

The team's first game was an away game. The second game was at home, at a nearby field. At halftime we had to gather together on the grass over to the side of the field because we didn't have a building or locker room. As I sat there with my teammates, I looked up and saw two familiar figures walking through the gate at the entrance. It was my dad and Virg! I grabbed my bag and ran behind the bleachers, quickly shedding my uniform and putting my street clothes back on. I tossed the bag aside and ran up to greet them. They both had smirks on their faces.

"We know you're playing, Dre," my father said.

I thought my dad was gonna kill me. I couldn't believe they had busted me like that. That shut down my football career.

During that time, I was starting to talk to my mother on the phone more and I would see her on occasion. It was still sporadic, but when I did see her, she was looking a lot better. I soaked up every second of her presence; without her and without my dad, I was craving parents. The voice in my head was telling me that maybe I could live with her. Perhaps on a subconscious level, I knew that I would have much less structure and much more freedom if I lived with her. My mom even provided me firsthand evidence of what it could be like. One day when she picked me up, I begged her to let me go to a party up the street that had been talked about all week. So she took me to the party and let me hang out for a few hours. She eventually brought me back to Millie and Virg without them ever finding out that we made a little pit stop. Honestly, I don't really think they would have cared, but I still never mentioned it. That night registered in my head. *Mom is gonna let me move around and do my thing.* Besides that, she was my mother and I just wanted to be with her.

During my sophomore year, after grappling with these thoughts for months, I finally worked up the nerve to discuss it with Virg.

"I don't know," I stammered, as he waited to see where I was going, "but I think I might want to go stay with my mom."

I know it was hurtful for him to hear me say that, but he didn't let it show. He just tried to talk me through it.

"Why do you want to do that?"

"I just miss my mom," I said.

There wasn't much he could say to that. How can you deny a boy who wants to be with his mom? Especially when my dad couldn't provide a stable living situation. In fact, I had started to build up a resentment toward him. I loved him, but I had some disdain, particu-larly when I thought about our years with him; I was now old enough to realize that he was often high around us, and those needles that I had found in his room were his. Drugs were once again the reason we weren't together. I never had the courage to confront him about how I felt.

Three years had passed since we were first dropped off at Millie and Virg's place. If my mom was now stable, I felt like it was time to move in with her. I was mainly in survival mode, just trying to deal with everything that had been thrown at me. I knew most of my friends had their mothers around, whether their dads were present or not. Children were supposed to be with their mothers. That's the way the world was supposed to work.

I even told Virg that Johnathan felt the same way—he wanted to be with his mother too. He wanted to be with his family up in Seattle, Washington—his mother, Cheryl, and his Grandma Barb (Cheryl's mother), who was the pillar of the family and the community. He wanted to leave our structured life, which was centered around boxing, and head up to Washington, where he knew he'd have more freedom too.

"If you want to go stay with your mother, I'm not gonna tell you that you can't," Virg said to me. "Your dad is totally against it, but I told him, 'Look, Duke, Dre hasn't been around his mom very much, you have to let him get this out of his system. You have to trust God with that.' But I'm going to be honest with you, Dre: you're going to go downhill."

When I heard that, I was offended. *What? Downhill?! What do you mean, downhill?!* I was at the age when you want what you want and you're not really open to any other perspective. I had been immersed in boxing for about five years; I was tired of the sport, tired of the grueling schedule, tired of the shackles. I wanted my mom. I wanted to be free.

FOUR

FEAR OF LOSING

It had taken a whole year before I stepped in the ring for my first amateur fight when I was ten years old. There were certain boxes that my dad and Virg needed to see checked before they would put me in a real match. They were constantly assessing my commitment to the sport; did I really love it the way I said I did? How was I responding when the competition got stiffer—would I turn or would I fight back? At that point I guess I had passed all their tests and answered all their questions. It was finally time to jump into the fire.

My first fight took place at the Santa Clara Police Activities League against a kid named Samuel Orozco. Samuel was from San Jose, just a few miles from Santa Clara, so he had a lot of people in the crowd, which made the scene a lot more intense for me. I had just a handful of people to support me—my dad, my brother, Uncle Bob, and Virg. That didn't really bother me because that's typically how we rolled, a small circle. A lot of my family members didn't agree with my dad letting me and my brother box; they thought he was crazy.

My opponent and I were evenly matched. We were both around the same height, with similar builds, though he might have been a little bit bigger.

We got there a couple hours before the fight, weighed in, checked in with the doctor, and I got handed a little white book. The book is your amateur boxing passport: they put all your medical information in there and the results of all your matches. It's basically like your amateur boxing DNA. Anytime coaches wanted to check to see how many fights an opponent had, they would check that book; it had all the information you needed. This was necessary on the amateur fight scene because, believe it or not, coaches would lie about how experienced their fighter really was to try to get them easy matches on the way up. This was the fight game showing its ugly colors even at the amateur level.

As the time for my first match grew closer, the nerves and anxiety grew. I could hear the crowd filing into the small venue, their voices growing louder and louder. I heard the announcements over the PA system that signaled the first bout was about to start. All of this felt a lot different than sparring. In these moments it's like your mind wants to drift and become a spectator of the event, but I had to learn as the fighter that I *was* the event. I couldn't be a spectator. I had to stay focused. I put my boxing shoes on first, my cup next, then my trunks and my tank top. When it was time to get my hands wrapped, I knew the moment of truth was getting closer. Virg was talking to me the whole time: "Hey, we're good. You've been battle hardened over the last year. You're ready for this."

Virg's voice in my ear was always a big help to me, reminding me that I did indeed belong there. I believed him; I knew this wasn't a game.

When I left the locker room and entered the arena, I started noticing a lot of eyeballs shift in my direction. They knew that my fight was next and I was up against the hometown kid. I made eye contact with my brother, Uncle Bob, and my pops, which lifted me up. At one hundred pounds, our fight was one of the first of the night. I headed to the ring, thinking about all the instructions and lessons I had gotten from my dad and Virg. "When you walk in there, you command that ring. You go around that whole ring, you look confident, feel confident. You've put the work in. Captivate the judges as soon as you get in there."

From day one, I was being groomed to take over, to look in charge, to make sure my body language was always right. All those things mattered.

"This is it, baby. This is what all the hard work was about."

Once the bell rang, all the nerves dissipated, and my instincts kicked in. It was time to fight. Once we got going, I saw that Samuel had a lot of skills; he was well taught. I felt I was landing more shots and cleaner shots. But amateur fights at that level are only three, one-minute rounds. They are really hard to score. They're so quick, that's why we called them smokers. What do you give more weight—who throws the most punches, who lands the most, or who is the most aggressive? After each round, the five judges around the ring hand in their scorecards. When the fight ends, all the scorecards are tallied up to see who the winner is. Once the final bell rang, I just knew I had won. Virg felt that way too. By the look on my father's face, he was in agreement with me and Virg. The emcee stood in the ring and announced the winner: Samuel Orozco!

I couldn't believe it. I lost my first fight. I was heartbroken. Devastated. I was such a competitive kid that the idea of losing had always killed me. Both my dad and Virg said the same thing: "You got robbed, Dre." It was the first time I had ever heard that expression. I would soon learn that it was far too prevalent in amateur boxing—the local kid would often get the nod, even if he didn't deserve it. This would happen at the local and state levels, even the national and international levels. Unfortunately, it was just baked into the amateur boxing system.

Virgil even went to the scorer's table to grill the judges about their decision.

He told them, "How in the world can you take this victory from him? He landed all the punches!"

They said, "Oh, well this is an amateur fight. The other kid threw more punches. Your kid landed more punches."

Virg responded, "Well isn't that what counts?"

After that, Virg began to tweak my style a little bit, slowly teaching me a pro style.

Not only was Samuel from that area, but he had already had two or three fights. Nobody knew who I was. In a close fight, they gave it to him. In my third fight I had the chance to fight Samuel again. This time I beat him. Ironically, Samuel and I would reconnect many years later and stay in touch. He's a good dude.

I hated losing my first fight, but the sting of that loss created a monster. I never wanted to lose again. I trained harder and felt more focused after my defeat. Maybe that was the point. I guess sometimes you have to take a step backward to get a running start, because I didn't lose again for a very long time.

After we got a few wins under my belt, Virg and my dad no longer had any trepidation. They were on the hunt for me to get as many fights as I could. I started to gain a buzz locally as I kept winning. I steadily worked my way toward the Nationals, winning at every step along the way. I won the Northern California championship and traveled to Southern California to face the SoCal champion. Everybody knew that winning in SoCal was the hardest part of the journey to get to the Nationals. They had the most kids in California and some of the best boxers. After winning the regionals, the last stop was the National Silver Gloves Championships in Lenexa, Kansas, where I would be fighting the best young boxers in the United States.

I was just as excited to see snow as I was for the competition. When we got off the plane in Kansas City, I couldn't believe all the snow I saw. I finally got a chance to sink my fingers into a pile of snow outside the hotel; it was cold and wetter than I expected.

Because the winters are so cold and long in Kansas, the hotel was set up so that all the activities were indoors—a pool, a gaming room, and a miniature golf course. Right away, Virg told me that this was a business trip. I needed to stay focused and get rest in my room. I couldn't spend a lot of time running around playing games in the hotel. Sheesh, any excitement and thoughts of being a kid that week got dashed quick. Back to reality. A lot of the kids were there to box but also there to play and have a good time. It was like a mini vacation for some—the only caveat was that you had to fight every day and keep your weight down so you wouldn't be overweight. Each day, depending on which weight class you fought in, you would have to hit that number until the tournament was over. To Virg's credit, he was right. I witnessed a bunch of kids ripping and running all week when they weren't in the ring. A lot of times, those kids would lose in the semifinals or the finals.

"You see that kid running around over there?" Virg said to me, pointing to one of the boxers. "Giving up all that energy. He needed it last night, and he lost. That's why."

I was a kid excited about traveling and seeing snow, but to Virg, we were there on a mission, and that was that. He wanted me to use my downtime to rest, to prepare for the next fight. When the brackets were set and we got the draw, Virg came back to the room and pointed out the name of a kid on the other side of the bracket—Curtis Stevens from Brownsville, New York. Curtis already had a cold reputation at ten years old. I knew that this kid was the biggest threat between me and my first national championship at one hundred pounds. Curtis Stevens's uncle, Andre Rozier, was downstairs at night with the other coaches making a strong case for his nephew to win the whole tournament.

"Man, y'all don't understand where Curtis comes from," Uncle Dre said to Virgil. "This kid grew up under Mike Tyson's doorstep. He's mean. Can't no kid stand up to Curtis's left hook, man!"

I don't know what Virg said in response to Uncle Dre's bold claims; I was only aware of what he told me when he came back to the room that night. "Dre, this kid from New York is supposed to be tough. His uncle is downstairs bragging about his power."

"Oh yeah?" I said.

"He's saying he grew up with Mike Tyson. Man, we don't care about that. He hasn't fought anybody like you. We just have to stay focused and get to those finals."

I nodded my head in approval. When I got a chance to be around the other boxers, it was interesting to see how the different teams were moving depending on where they were from. The Philly cats moved militant—they all wore kufis and their team was called "Concrete Jungle." I never saw them playing around the hotel. They played no games, and all those boys could fight. New York kids always had the most up-to-date fashion, and they always seemed older than their age. Most of the NY crew could rumble; they were respected among our peers. The Ohio fighters were the wildest of the bunch. Somebody always got in trouble from Ohio at the national tournaments, and it wasn't always the fighters. A lot of times it was the coaches too. The

Ohio boys had the most swag; it seemed like everybody from that state could fight and they would let you know about it. They talked that talk, and most of the time they backed it up. I can't forget about Michigan. They not only could fight, but they were also tough. Michigan coaches loved saying, "We gonna leave body bags out here, man."

I just watched it all without saying anything. All that bragging wasn't my style. I was confident and I knew we were going to have to fight. I never felt the need to announce I was coming; I just wanted to show up. But I was amused when I realized that they thought California kids were soft. Maybe it was because they thought Cali was just about Los Angeles and Hollywood. Clearly, they didn't know anything about Northern California; they didn't know anything about the Bay Area, Hayward, and Oakland.

As the week went on, Virg was always on the ground at the three-ring site where we fought, watching other kids fight, talking to coaches, getting any information he could on my future opponents. I was winning my fights by outboxing my opponents. Curtis was knocking dudes out, one after another. He was bragging about Tyson, but he was looking like him a little bit too: short and stocky with a mean left hook. Uncle Dre was right about what he said Curtis would do. As we approached the end of the five-day tournament, it became apparent that we were going to face off in the finals. Virg constantly worked on my psyche, preparing me for war.

"See, this is the thing, baby. He ain't fought nobody like you. They can come with this Brownsville thing and stuff like that, but we're from Oakland. And they're gonna see."

Remember, we're talking about ten-year-olds. The pressure was real, but this became normal to us as young fighters. You either get with the program, or you get stepped on. I didn't want to get stepped on. I knew my folks back in the Bay Area were looking for updates after every fight.

"How'd Dre do?"

"Did Andre win?"

When Curtis and I finally met, I discovered quickly that his power was the real deal. It was the hardest I'd ever been hit at that point in my career. Dude was just heavy-handed, the type of punch that you feel even when you block it. But I beat him, and I beat him good; I was just a better boxer than him. (I ended up beating him two more times throughout our amateur careers.) That was a huge moment for me. Virg and my dad knew for certain that I was something special after the Stevens fight. It wasn't a local thing anymore or even a state thing. I was the best ten-year-old fighter in the United States at one hundred pounds. I was so excited when I got handed my prize: a championship belt (blue with little silver pendants), two silver gloves that said "1996 Silver Gloves, Lenexa, Kansas," and a silver champions jacket. Every amateur boxer in the country wanted that silver jacket and that blue belt. That's what we talked about all year, winning the National Silver Gloves. I always wanted a championship belt, and now I had one. It signified that I was the best fighter in the country at my age and weight.

After winning the Nationals, both my confidence and my reputation grew. I wanted to win more of these. When I entered the ring for local matches, I could hear the whispers. "Oh, that's Ward right there. He just won the Nationals." You win the Nationals and you get instant clout. To a limited extent, my success was now even reaching my friends.

"Hey Dre, my mom said you were in the newspaper," one of my boys said.

"Wow, that's cool, bro!" another said.

I was living in two different worlds: a normal kid some days and a boxer who had to train and eat right on other days.

Looking back, I realize how we never really celebrated our victories.

As soon as I won the Nationals or any other fight, we enjoyed it for a week or so. Then we set our sights on the next fight.

"Hey, we got to put that behind us. Time to get back to work," my dad and Virg would always say.

We never counted how many national titles we won; we just cared about winning. My brother, Johnathan, won a few as well. It took him a few years longer to get there. He seemed like he always had a tough bracket and would lose before he got to the finals. But he picked up his share of belts. He was always a little bit bigger, a little bit taller and heavier, so there was never a chance we would fight each other. I always felt like my brother had more natural ability than me, I just loved it more than he did.

I could tell that Virg was always concerned about me and my brother burning out. He would hear stories from other coaches about young boxers who would get burned out and quit. He didn't want that to be us. So every once in a while, he would give us a few days off.

"You worked hard this week—you can take off Saturday and Sunday," he'd say. Or he'd say, "Go see what's up with your folks at Sparks Way," which was one of my spots to hang out.

Virg did a great job throughout my career of knowing when he should pull back and give me a break. As I got older, he would have to force me to take breaks because I'd never do it if it was left to me. I would mess it up every time and overtrain. I needed him to be my extra set of eyes. I can't tell which was stronger, my fear of losing or my deep desire to win. I do know they worked in tandem, and they worked for me. That fear and desire made me push myself to the point of exhaustion, and at times to the point of throwing up. I didn't want anyone to work harder than me, and I never wanted to lose ever again.

It became apparent to our friends that Johnathan and I weren't like the other kids; we didn't have a normal kid lifestyle. They knew there were times when they didn't see us, when we were travelling to boxing tournaments. But they never really knew the details of what we were up to. I liked it better that way. I felt my life was a little weird; it didn't resemble anybody else's life that I knew except for my brother's—and even he didn't have the same level of commitment I did. Who else was being trained in this sport of violence, who sparred against other people three days a week, who came home with headaches sometimes because of taking hard shots? Who else did this? Knowing this, a part of me was a little embarrassed by it all. I preferred to keep the boxing as a secret part of my life, tucked away. I would only really discuss the topic when it was brought up and I had no choice. When people heard that I boxed, they'd always look at me with a strange reaction that let me know it wasn't normal.

FIVE

NORTH OAKLAND

Even with Virg's words, "You're going to go downhill," ringing in my head, living with my mom again gave me exactly what I always wanted in the beginning: the love and affection that I had craved since the previous times I'd lived with her. I missed waking up every day and seeing her clean and sober, cleaning the house, making dinner, doing all the things you see a mother doing. This always gave me peace. My mother was happy too.

My mom was a good mother to me and my siblings. She was always a lot of fun, loved music, and could sing. She fussed from time to time like any mother might do, but at her core, she's always had a sweet spirit about her. But if you crossed her or her babies, she wasn't anyone to play with. I get my big, bright smile from my mother's side of the family. That's something I've always loved to see on her face. Like most people, when my mother smiles and laughs, I know she's happy and at peace, which is all I've ever wanted for her.

As my mother's youngest child, I have always hated to see her struggle, and I carried the burden to want to save her. Over the years, I've accepted that it's far too great a burden to carry and that I ultimately don't have the power to save my mother. That's God's business, and though he has the power to save her, she has to want to be saved. I was faced with this reality once again as I started to notice subtle changes in my mom's behavior and her attitude.

When my mom was well, she was always a neat freak. Whenever she started to slip, the house would slip along with her. The apartment was getting messy, the carpet was dirty, and my mother didn't seem to care. She was starting to get that look again. I didn't know it at the time, but right around the corner from our apartment complex was the neighborhood dope house. My mother eventually found her way there. Things began to fall apart.

My commute to Hayward High School from North Oakland was becoming more of a burden. Nobody was on my back, making sure I made it to school, so it became less of a priority for me. At that age most kids need some level of authority or they have the potential to go astray. I'd get on the Bay Area Rapid Transit (BART) train in North Oakland and do the hour-long ride, but once I got to Hayward I'd start catting off with my boys, get distracted, and find myself not going to class. I'd tell myself, *I'll just pull up to third period.* But third period would come and I still hadn't shown up. There were other times when I would make it to school, but as soon as I arrived, inevitably one of my homeboys would ask me, "I've got some weed. You wanna smoke?" If they caught me on the right day, I'd be out of there. I'd hop in the car, always looking over my shoulder for the police. We could get suspended or go to jail if we ran into a cop. Once I was high, there was no need to go back to class. I might not get back to Oakland until eight or nine o'clock, but my mother would have nothing to say.

Eventually the slippage in attendance and grades caught up to me.

Hayward sent me away to a "continuation school." That was the place they sent the bad kids. There were a few teachers and a counselor named Mr. Green at the school who seemed to care and tried to get through to me, but I wasn't fully receptive. The Hayward Unified School District didn't seem to have the infrastructure in place to help kids succeed when they were falling between the cracks like me. But honestly, I don't think it would have mattered. Even if I was at the best school in the world, I'm not sure I would have been receptive to any help they were offering. I believe the years of pain and trauma, coupled with my teenage rebellion, were finally catching up to me, and made it easy for me to reject any authority in my life and refuse the help that was extended to me. By the beginning of my senior year, I stopped going to school.

Boxing was no longer getting the best version of me either. I didn't want to do it anymore. I started drinking and dabbling with hard drugs. When I look back at pictures from that time period, my eyes look cold, almost lifeless. I was lost. I was hurting. I was numb. I was on the verge of crashing out and ruining my life. My mother was in no position to help me. By that point, she was lost again too.

I started to sell crack to keep a few dollars in my pocket to make up the difference for what my mom couldn't do at the time. It wasn't like I envisioned myself as some rising kingpin. I never saw myself running a block; I just wanted to make some bread. There was a dude on the block that we'll call OG Juice. Juice was a professional criminal. He was street savvy and had a lot of game. For some reason, Juice embraced me and looked out for me. Eventually I discovered that he sold my mama dope, but I didn't know at the time. Anytime he and I would do business, it would be when my mother wasn't there. Juice knew I didn't cook dope so he would sell me what he had already bagged up, sometimes twenty to thirty rocks at a time. He always gave me a slight discount so that I could make a profit.

I sold on the move, up and down blocks around my neighborhood, either walking or on a bike. I didn't have a gun nor did I have a designated block. Movement and being aware of my surroundings at all times were my means of staying safe and out of the way. I learned to watch and identify every car that passed by, and I kept a mental log just in case a car doubled back. This could be an undercover narcotics officer or a jacker, somebody looking to rob you for your dope.

I would rotate my bundle between my pocket and my mouth. If I kept rocks in my mouth for too long, my mouth would go numb. If the police pulled up, I could just swallow the dope—though I never thought I would actually have to do that. If I saw a knock—our name for a crack addict—coming my way, we would make eye contact; they would give a nod, as if to ask, "Do you have it?" I would give myself a few seconds to read the play. *Do I recognize this person? Do they look hot? Should I serve them?* If I calculated wrong, I was going to prison for a very long time. They would whisper the desired amount they wanted, I would spit it out of my mouth, and we would exchange money for drugs. I would take the money, look over my shoulder, and keep it moving. I didn't roll with a crew and I didn't really have a strategy selling drugs, so I never felt entirely comfortable—with good reason.

One night I was in front of my apartment building on Fifty-Fifth and Market and a dude we'll call Big Dub pulled up. Dub sold dope in my neighborhood, but I didn't realize that he considered my block part of his territory. I usually tried to stay on the move, but on this night for some reason I decided to post up in one place: in front of the building where I lived.

"Hey, blood, what's up?" Dub said.

"What's up?" I answered.

"What you out here doing?" he asked.

"Nothing, bruh. I'm just posted up."

"I hope you not out here selling dope or nothin', bro. You know this is my spot, right?"

"No, I don't know what you talking about, bro. Like I said, I'm just postin'. I ain't selling no dope."

In fact, I had a pocketful of dope. But what I didn't have was a strap. If he wanted to get spunky, I wasn't prepared. He pulled off without saying another word. I let out a deep exhale. I don't know if he saw through me and knew I was lying to him. From that encounter, I knew that he was going to keep watching me. I wasn't really consistent with the dope selling. He might see me moving around the neighborhood, but it was probably hard for him to put his finger on what I was doing.

A couple months later, the streets caught up with Dub—he got shot in the head right in front of his house on Market Street, two blocks from my house. In retrospect, moments like that encounter with Big Dub allowed me to see all the times that God had mercy on me. He kept me safe despite the way I was living at that time. Deep down I knew I wasn't fully committed to the street life. It's like when I talk to a boxer about the boxing life, I want to know, "Are you in it for the money? Are you in it for the fame? Or do you just like the idea of what comes with being a champion?" I can read a fighter with ease, gauge their level of commitment. I think on the streets some dudes could peep that about me. I'm sure they knew I wasn't fully living it. It would have been too easy for me to lose my life right there on the block, just like Dub did.

The dudes I was running with knew I was a boxer; they heard about my accomplishments. I had a reputation. But they didn't know how deep I was involved in the sport or how I was squandering it all. In my mind, I was no longer that guy—the boxing stuff was in the rearview mirror. They knew me as young Dre, or Madeline's son. They didn't know me as a fighter. My mom would always brag about me being a boxer, but I could tell they didn't really get it. Probably because

I had one foot in boxing and one foot in the streets. Nobody on the streets was saying, "Yo, you the next one, bro. We got to protect you." That's the kind of thing you see with a young basketball or football phenom. In my case, maybe if I was living the life of an athlete, if they saw me going to the gym, running regularly, they might have taken that position. But what they saw was a young kid on the street corner, hustling, selling drugs and making bad decisions.

When my mother started slipping again, we would get into these blowups. I would accuse her and she would constantly deny it.

"I'm only smoking a little weed—what's wrong with that?" she said.

"Mama, you ain't just smoking weed. I know that look."

"Well, you can think what you want to think!"

"Naw, Mom, I know what I'm looking at."

Another time I found broken pieces of pipe in her room. I brought the evidence to her, but still she denied.

"Oh, Shanae was over here—that's hers."

"Mom, what are you talkin' about? I ain't no fool! I've been through this before. I'm looking at how you're movin'. I'm looking at this house."

"All you want to do is blame me every time you think I'm back using!"

By now, I had developed a keen eye for spotting a drug user—an expertise I never wanted.

The brutal thing about crack is that it supersedes everything else in your life—your dignity, your family, and truth. Everything gets drowned out by the desire to want to get high. With Mom, it was especially painful because she had beaten this addiction multiple times before; God had answered her prayers and delivered her. She would be fine. But that was the pattern of my life—Mom is good, then she would relapse; Dad is good, Dad would relapse. Over and over. I wasn't a kid anymore. I was older now and had years of experience studying both of my parents. I wasn't going to just fall apart. My heart had hardened; though it would still hurt, I wouldn't show it. I became numb. I remained in this state by abusing drugs and alcohol and distancing myself.

Virg wasn't letting my drift go unaddressed. He was getting at me about the way I was living. Virg lived his life like he was playing chess. He would see and hear things about me but wouldn't reveal what he knew until he was ready to drop the hammer and confront me. But I was pushing back, not receiving what he was trying to give me. I was moving away from him. I was able to clean myself up for certain periods to get ready for the big tournaments. Virg would track me down and get me to focus for a four- or five-week period.

"Come on, we need this, Dre. Gotta get focused."

I would be able to stay away from the streets and get myself together long enough to go win another national title. I was the number one ranked amateur in the country, but I was still missing a lot of tournaments too. When you're on the amateur boxing circuit, you're fighting all throughout the year. A few times I did enough to qualify for the Nationals but then didn't show up. A week or a few days before it was time to leave, I would come up with an excuse.

"Aw, man, Virg, uh, my back hurts. I don't know if I can go."

Another time I said it was my knee, or I would just disappear altogether and leave him hanging. Looking back on this period is shameful, but it goes to show what kind of person you can become if you allow yourself to drift too far.

My lifestyle was showing up in the boxing gym. There were times when I would be in the streets all night, drinking and smoking weed, and Virg would call me and expect me to be in the gym the next morning, ready to spar. I would show up, knowing that I wasn't at my best. Everybody in the gym still looked at me like an Olympic hopeful, but I didn't feel like one. I would be strong for two or three rounds and then I would start to feel nauseous. The poison I had consumed the night before was coming up whether I wanted it to or not. I would run to the corner and throw up in a bucket. Virg could smell the alcohol on my breath and would give me this deep look of disappointment and shake his head. I would finish the sparring session by coasting to the final bell, uninterested in exerting too much effort for fear I would throw up again. Virg would take off my sparring equipment, barely saying anything more than, "Son, you've got to get yourself together. You don't have much time left."

I blew off the National Golden Gloves in 2002 in Las Vegas. James Prince, who is a boxing manager and the CEO of Rap-A-Lot Records, flew to Vegas to see me fight. He was disappointed that I didn't show up, but Prince didn't leave it there. To this day, I still don't know how Virg tracked me down and got me on the phone. I was at a trap house tucked away. Prince wanted to know why I wasn't at the Nationals. I began to tell Prince everything I had going on in my life and I expected him to back away, but Prince didn't hesitate when he said, "We're gonna take care of all those misdemeanor problems. We just need to get you back in the ring."

He wasn't talking about a police record. He was referencing the issues that I was dealing with.

Prince and I wouldn't speak again for several months, but that conversation left an impression on me. He was the first manager to go out of his way and run me down to express that he wanted to do business. I respected that.

Virg was still in my ear constantly, trying to get me to see the light. He would appeal to me on a spiritual level, telling me the devil wanted to take me out but God loved me. He talked to me about the generational curses of drug use that existed in my family. He would tell me that I was giving in to the same forces that my mother and father battled for much of their lives. And he also took it to the streets.

"Brother, let me tell you something," he said. "You out here fakin'."

I was angry when I heard that. "What you mean, fakin'?! Ain't nothin' fake about me!"

"Look, you out there playing and roaming around like you're established in the streets. You ain't making no moves in the streets. You ain't no kingpin. You ain't running no block. You just running around here with a bunch of dudes getting high. That's what you're doing. You ain't really about that life."

"Man, you trippin', Virg," I responded.

"Let me tell you something. If you ain't ready to sell your soul to the devil right now and be willing to kill somebody, if you ain't ready to be killed, you fakin' out here in these streets."

Even though what he said angered me, it also shook me up. I had never really thought about the level of treachery that it takes to survive in the streets until that moment. But he was right. I played it off in front of him, but when I got away from him I sat with that for a long time. The reality was I wasn't trying to kill nobody, and I definitely wasn't trying to be killed. Again, it was like boxing—you can't go into a big fight without embracing and acknowledging the fact that you might get knocked out. You're telling yourself it ain't gonna happen—you're gonna win this fight. But you're ready for the worst-case scenario. It's the same in the streets. That's the point that Virg was trying to make, because that's the type of individuals you're dealing with.

Still, I was young and rebellious. Virg's words alone weren't going to do it. But in the midst of my rebellion, I had two experiences that finally managed to penetrate my hard head and begin to break me down.

I was standing in front of a liquor store on Fifty-Sixth and Market as I sold a couple rocks to this lady. As soon as I finished the transaction, I had a clear thought pop into my head, almost like a voice talking to me: *How are you going to ask me to take away your mother's*

addiction but you're serving somebody else's mama crack? You're poison-
ing your community, but you want me to deliver your mother?

I was stunned. I felt shame creeping in. I knew it was God showing me how I was acting like a straight hypocrite. My mother was a block away with an active crack addiction that I was desperate to see shut down, yet I was enabling somebody else's mom in her addiction. This moment revealed to me how desensitized I had become, but it also showed that I wasn't too far gone and my conscience was still active. The lady I served drugs to was wearing a long overcoat and a beanie on her head, and she didn't have any teeth. Clearly, she was deep in the throes of her addiction. I felt convicted for my selfishness, being so blinded by the money and the lure of the streets that I would have the audacity to pray for the taste to be taken from my mother's mouth as I fed the taste to someone else's. It was God chipping away at me, deliver-ing another timely warning. Often, warning comes before destruction.

I felt the warnings, but I still wasn't ready to surrender my life to God. I was still out there, but now I found myself being a little more careful in my movements, keeping my eyes peeled for dudes like Big Dub and for the police. I was aware of the California mandatory min-imums at that time for selling drugs. Usually ten or fifteen rocks even with no record would get you at least three years in state prison. I just missed that bus ride to San Quentin.

I got hit with another warning a few months later, two blocks from where I lived. I was riding my bike slowly, looking for knocks, holding about twelve rocks in my mouth. When I turned a corner on the bike, a cop car pulled up behind me. The car shined its floodlights at me. I felt my stomach drop.

"Hey, you! Stop!" The voice was amplified over the car's loudspeaker.

I stopped my bike. My mouth was filled with a bunch of crack cocaine. I had to make a quick decision. *Swallow the rocks or go to prison.* I started to swallow them one by one as I set my bike down slowly, trying to buy a little time. The rocks were double bagged, so I felt like I was safe enough to swallow a few. I slowly turned around as I could hear the cop approaching me. I swallowed a few more rocks, enough to talk without sounding crazy.

"What's the problem?" I said, carefully controlling my voice.

"Where you going?" the cop said.

"Sir, I'm just riding my bike. I'm not bothering anybody. I live around the corner."

"Yeah, but I see you riding around looking suspicious," he said.

I was trying to talk without the rest of the rocks falling out of my mouth. It was too late to try to swallow any more of them. Even as I was talking, I was feeling a growing sense of panic about the ones I already swallowed—while fighting the fear that I could be arrested for possession.

He moved closer to me, shining the flashlight in my face.

"You ain't doin' nothin', huh?" the cop asked me, watching my face closely.

"Man, I'm just heading home." Trying to back him off of me, I started to get bolder. I added, "You want to follow me to my house? I live around the corner—what's the problem?"

"I'm just checking, man. Calm down," he said.

He studied me for another minute or so, then turned around and headed back to his car. As I climbed on the bike, I felt around in my mouth. I had swallowed all but two of them. I spit those two out and put them in my pocket. *I just swallowed ten crack rocks!* The panic rose in my body as I pumped my legs and raced home as fast as I could.

"Mama! Mama!" I screamed when I busted through our front door. "I just swallowed ten rocks!"

"What you mean?" she said when she saw me.

"I was out there trying to make some money . . . This cop got behind me!"

I knew that I had to get them out of my system as quickly as possible. If the acid in your stomach made them bust open before you could use the bathroom, you could overdose and die.

I thanked God that OG Juice had done what he was supposed to do and double-bagged the rocks. But even with the double bags, I knew I was in a life-or-death situation.

I ran to the liquor store and bought chocolate Ex-Lax. I quickly downed three bars of the Ex-Lax before I even got back home. I sat on the toilet immediately but nothing happened—obviously the Ex-Lax wasn't going to work that fast. I was thoroughly spooked. Logic had flown out the window. At any moment I could have a heart attack or overdose. I just had to wait it out, terrified the whole time, thinking wild thoughts.

"Boy, I can't believe you out there selling dope!" my mother said. "You know, you can get yourself killed out there in them streets."

"I know, Mom. But how you gonna tell me what I need to be doing when you out there doing drugs?"

That wasn't the first time we had had this argument. We went back and forth for a while. Eventually I moved away from her and started talking to God.

"Lord, please don't let me die like this."

I went to the toilet again. The Ex-Lax was starting to do its job. Real street hustlers go in the toilet to fetch out their dope, clean it off, and hit the block again to go sell it. I wasn't thinking about that dope nor the money I had just lost either.

The warnings were piling up and I didn't know how many I had left.

My life was spiraling out of control, but when that dope got flushed, my drug-selling days got flushed down the toilet right along with it.

SIX

DIAMOND IN
THE ROUGH

After my brother moved to Washington to live with his mother, I really missed him. We did everything together. I felt lost without him around. Every time I talked to him on the phone, it sounded like he was having the time of his life—a lot more fun than I was having.

"Bro, I need to come visit you, man!" I told him. I wanted to see what all the fuss was about up there in Seattle. I went up in the late spring, before the start of summer vacation. Johnathan was planning a party at his mother's house that weekend. I got there on a Friday and went to meet him at his high school. I walked around campus and spoke to a few of his friends—and of course I was checking out the girls. I considered myself a good-looking kid and it was evident that the girls liked me, but I was shy at the same time. A lot of girls back at Hayward High thought I was stuck-up because I didn't go out of my way to talk to them; maybe some of that was true but that wasn't the full story. It was easier for me to fall back and wait for girls to show some interest in me before I would make any kind of move. That was my strategy. My brother was the opposite—he was extremely outgoing and would approach a girl without a second thought.

Johnathan had been prepping the girls at his school for my arrival. I'm not sure what he said about me, but there was a crowd of girls waiting when I got to the school. I loved it. But one particular girl who was standing away from the crowd caught my eye. She was beautiful— caramel-colored skin and big, pretty brown eyes. Her hair was in a curly ponytail; I saw her smile and could see that she had braces on her teeth. She was all the way across the courtyard doing her own thing with some of her friends, but my eyes were locked on her like a laser.

"Hey, man, who's that?" I asked Johnathan.

He looked over and saw where my gaze was pointed.

"Oh, that's Tiffiney Smith," he said.

"Oh yeah? Go see what's up with her," I said.

As Johnathan went over to talk to her, I watched nervously. He invited her to his party and she told him she might be there. When he came back, I knew I had to ask him about one thing: her feet.

"She good, bro," he said.

"Are you sure?"

"Yeah, she good."

I'm not sure where it came from, but I've always had a thing about a girl's feet. I just could not go out with a girl with ugly feet. I dumped a girl in sixth grade because I didn't like her toes. I was always interested in shoes, even as a little boy. When I met someone, the first thing I would do is look at their shoes, then I would look up and greet them. Don't ask me how the shoe obsession evolved to pretty feet, but somehow it did.

Tiffiney showed up at my brother's party that night with a few of

DIAMOND IN THE ROUGH

her girlfriends. I was excited to see her; I just knew she was there to see me. I felt a little self-conscious because I hadn't had money to get my braids redone before I went to Washington. I was looking rough, just like a dude who was running around the streets of Oakland. Luckily it was kinda dark in the garage, where the party was being held. I thought I might have some action with Tiffiney, but she was giving me the impression she wasn't interested.

"What's up? Do you want to dance?" I said when I walked over to her. But she was resistant and a bit standoffish. I was already stepping outside of my comfort zone by initiating a conversation with her. When I got those vibes from her, I fell back. I don't chase. To save face, I shifted my focus to the other girls in the room, some of the same ones who were excited to see me earlier that day. If she wasn't interested, I wasn't either.

Andre's brother and I had two classes together, psychology and PE, and we also had friends in common, so sometimes we would talk. One day he started telling me about his brother, letting me know Andre and I had a lot in common and he thought we would really like each other.

Okay, this brother's in California, so who cares? I thought. *Why are you telling me this?*

And then one day Johnathan pulled up at school with his brother and told me he was having a birthday party. He said he wanted me and Andre to meet. Once again I was thinking, *Okay, whatever.*

"But wait!" he said. "I need to check your feet."

"Whaaattt?!"

I just happened to be wearing sandals that day. This guy actually looked down at my feet.

"Okay, yeah. You have nice feet, you're good," he said

What the heck? I thought that was the craziest thing I'd ever heard.

That was my first encounter with Andre before I actually met him. It was not the greatest first impression. As I looked across the courtyard I watched a light-skinned guy step out of the car. I saw Johnathan, so I figured that was "the brother." He leaned up against the side of the car and looked around, his confidence brimming like he owned the place. I thought, *Who does this guy think he is?* In an instant, I saw a bunch of girls swarming. From what I could tell from where I was, which was pretty far away, he seemed cute. But the girls were going crazy, which turned me off right away. I think they were excited because he was a new guy. Johnathan had been telling me about Dre for weeks, so I knew exactly who he was. But I didn't want to be part of the flock swarming around him. All of a sudden, Johnathan ran up to me and said, "My brother is here."

"Oh yeah?" I said—as if I didn't know.

"I want you to come to my party tonight so y'all can kick it," he said. At this point I was semi-interested. "Just come. You're gonna have a good time."

I rolled up to Johnathan's party that night with a few of my girls. The party was in a garage, at the house of a guy named Jim who Johnathan's mother was dating. When I saw Andre, there were still a bunch of girls around him. I still had no interest in joining the flock. Andre slowly made his way over to me. Up close, I could see that he had his hair braided—but the braids didn't look good, like they had been in a few weeks too long. He was looking a little rough. I wondered, *What's up with his hair?*

"Do you want to dance?" he said.

"No," I answered—the first word I ever said to him.

And then I proceeded to dance with just about every other guy at the party. I'm not even sure why I did that. I could tell when he came back over to talk to me that he was annoyed.

"Oh, so that's what you're gonna do?" he said. "You just gonna dance with everybody else and not dance with me."

I shrugged. I decided I had had enough of this party, so I left, well before it was over. It wasn't like I had some complicated master plan to seduce Dre by playing hard to get or something. I was only fifteen; I was just being me. I also had a boyfriend at the time and wasn't interested in some random long-distance thing.

Johnathan called me the next day and asked if I wanted to come over and hang at the house.

"For what?" I asked.

"Man, we just gonna hang out and smoke."

I paused. "Okay," I said.

I brought my best friend with me. I got my boyfriend to drive us over there. He was a few years older than me, so he had a car.

"Wait, so what are you doing?" he asked.

"I'm just hanging out with some friends." Little did he know he was driving me to go see another guy.

When we got there, Andre had put on a durag, so his braids were covered up. Johnathan kept nudging us to go talk. So that's what we did. My friends and I showed up late morning and I stayed there until late that night, getting to know Dre. We talked about our interests, our musical tastes, things like that. At one point he told me, "Oh yeah, I box."

"Really? That's cool. I play basketball," I answered. I had no idea.

I liked him, but I was thinking, *Hey, where is this really gonna go? He doesn't live here; he's from California. So what are we really doing?*

The following weekend, Andre was back again. That's when things got a lot more intense. We were intimate for the first time. I wrestled again with the fact that he was going back home to California, wondering how far this relationship could go. But then I settled within myself, *Whatever we do, it's fine, since he's just going to leave. No one else will know.* But then he kept coming back.

Tiffiney

When I visited Tiffiney that next weekend, we spent a lot of time talking about our lives and our backgrounds. I found out her biological father wasn't around and she had been raised by her mother and her stepfather, Billy, who was the biological dad of her sister, Tasha. Both of Tiffiney's parents were in the military, so she had spent many years living in Germany as a child. Her stepfather was a tough disciplinarian, but he had recently passed away. Tiffiney always tells me that if Billy had been alive at the time, we probably never would have met. As I shared my story with her, we realized we had many things in common. After hearing her story, my interest in her grew.

At one point that evening, we started smoking weed. We were kissing and getting closer and we wound up being intimate that night. After we were done and she had left, I went into the garage, where we had the party the weekend before, and I sat on the pool table with my mind spinning. I was worried about us not using any protection. But that thought was soon gone. When she came over the next day, we were intimate again.

I felt a strong connection between us. Even though we had just met, it felt like we had known each other for years. It was hard for me to leave on Sunday.

"I'm gonna come back," I told her.

"You ain't coming back!" she said.

But I did. I became a frequent flyer on the Southwest Airlines corridor between Oakland and Seattle. I was breaking my neck to get up there, spending my last dollar. I was in love. When I was younger, Virg always used to tell me, "You ain't gonna be no player, man. You're a one-woman man!" I have no idea how he knew that about me when I was a little kid. But Virg often had a prophetic voice as he spoke into my life. Again and again, he would say things that eventually came true. He even wrote down a lot of what he envisioned about my life in a journal; he was accurate about a lot of it. Gold medal, becoming a world champion, broadcaster, and Hall of Famer. It's all in the journal, written years before any of these things came to pass.

Tiffiney was beyond beautiful, but there was something else about her that was different than all the girls I had ever been around. She was extremely smart, and her personality was infectious. When I couldn't afford a plane ticket, I would run down to the Greyhound station on San Pablo Street in North Oakland and jump on a bus for a twenty-hour ride. Yes, it was that serious to me. I would tell my mother and Virg that I was going to visit Johnathan, but really I'd be going to see her. As I got to know her better, I grew fascinated by her background. She didn't grow up in the hood. After moving back to the U.S. from Germany, she lived in a nice house in a mostly white, middle-class neighborhood. She had just watched Billy battle cancer and dwindle away in less than a year. That pushed her mother, Remel, into a midlife crisis, dating again and trying to figure life out. Tiffiney went into a serious rebellion. On the surface I saw this beautiful girl with a great personality, but underneath she had a lot of trauma and anger that was undealt with. Tiffiney and her mother had frequent conflict. She was fighting in school, fighting with teachers. She was a straight-A student, but she was in and out of juvenile hall and continued to find herself in trouble. Her mother had even called the police on her because she didn't know how to handle Tiffiney. There were times when I was in town and her mother would tell her she couldn't leave the house, but she would still come see me.

"Didn't your mom say you couldn't leave the house?" I asked her.

"She did. But my mom left, so I just left."

I was out in the streets and rebellious myself, but I knew deep down Tiffiney was tripping, and I wanted to protect her. I wasn't intimidated by her rebellion. I saw a girl who was hurting, who was crying out. That attracted me to her more. Even though I wasn't a model citizen, I kept thinking, *I can help you. You've got a lot of potential.* It certainly was hypocritical at times, but that's how I was wired. I never really wanted my brother or Tiffiney to use any drugs or get involved in anything too crazy in my presence. I wasn't being fake; I was behaving more out of a sense of protection. Whereas Tiffiney was impulsive at times, I was always thinking two steps ahead about the consequences. Where I came from and growing up the way I was raised, you better learn to think before you act. A wrong move could cost you your life or your freedom.

Calling Tiffiney long-distance back then was expensive and we burned through more calling cards than I can remember. Any chance I got, I would call her on the school phone in the football locker rooms. It was free, and I could call long-distance. One day, I called Tiffiney right before I was about to go to practice. She picked up the phone right away.

"Hey, Tiff, what's up? You good?"

"Dre," she said. "I'm pregnant."

I almost dropped the phone. All I had ever heard from my dad and Virg was them telling me that if I got somebody pregnant as a teenager, or before my career took off, that my career could be over. That's all I heard. It had been repeated so often that it was like a commandment. I was shook. I was only sixteen. To me, hearing that news meant my boxing career had just ended. I didn't have any money and I had no idea how to take care of a child. My career flashed before my eyes. But then I snapped back and realized a few things about myself.

I'm not a runner, and I knew I was going to be there for the mother of my child.

"We gonna be alright," I said. "We gonna figure it out."

I didn't know how; I just knew that we would. I wasn't raised to run from my responsibilities.

SEVEN

ROCK BOTTOM

I was not looking forward to telling my father I had gotten a girl pregnant. I just knew he was going to go off on me after all the times he
had warned me about it. But when I finally worked up the courage, I
was surprised by his reaction.

"Okay, man, we gotta figure this out," he said. He appeared calm.
No yelling, no cussing. I could tell he was shocked, but he decided to
focus on the details. *Who is she? When did this happen?* I tried to give
him as much information as I could without providing too many gory
details. What I got most of all from him was a sense of his disappointment. He didn't blow up at me, but I had let him down. I'm sure he
blamed himself. He was never a fan of me going to Washington or me
living with my mother. In his mind, this was a consequence of that.

During the pregnancy, I tried to get up to Washington as often as I
could, but there still were long stretches when Tiffiney and I didn't see
each other. I was still a sixteen-year-old high school student, trying to
stay on top of my schoolwork, and a national champion boxer, trying

to stay focused so I could make it to the Olympics. I remember burning through so many long-distance calling cards I bought down at the
liquor store—220-minute cards, 130-minute cards; I loved talking to
Tiffiney on the phone and phone calls were all we had.

When I was in Washington, I interacted with her mom, Remel, but
I knew she wasn't a big fan of mine. I was this knucklehead, rebellious
kid with braids from California who got her daughter pregnant. When
I was at her house, we were decent, but I could always tell she felt a way
about me. And I don't blame her. In her shoes, I would have too. To her
credit, she tolerated my presence. Neither the mother nor the daughter
was impressed by my boxing accomplishments. I had told Tiffiney about
all the national championships I had won and that I would eventually
become a world champion. Her reaction was along the lines of, "Oh, that's
cool, Dre." But it clearly didn't register. This was before Google, so all she
really had to go on was the word of this teenage boy trying to impress her.

You already know from Dre what I always told him, that if my dad
had still been alive, I probably never would have met him. My dad
was very old school and regimented. Dating? Oh, we're not even
talking about that until you're eighteen—*that* kind of environment.

Throughout the summer of 2000, Dre was coming up to see me
as often as he could.

At one point I realized that I had missed my period. I was alarmed
to find out I was pregnant.

What am I going to do? My mom is gonna kill me!

When Andre called me from his school phone, I was afraid to tell
him, scared of what his reaction would be. But when I told him, he
said all the right things, that we would get through this together. We
were having a baby and that meant I had to tell my mother.

Since it's cold in Washington most of the time, I knew I had at least another month or maybe even two where I could wear sweatshirts and hoodies that would cover me up and no would know my condition. But I couldn't cover up forever.

I finally got up the nerve. My mother was in the kitchen when I told her, "Mom, I need to talk to you. I need you to sit down."

"Sit down?" she said, worry crossing her face. "Are you pregnant?"

Why is that the first thing you're gonna say?

She responded with a lot of yelling and cussing, telling me I had ruined my life and that I was out in the streets with some random boy from California who knocked me up. That I was so much smarter than that. The end result? She kicked me out of the house.

After a few months, my mother and I connected again. She came to my doctor appointment to find out the gender of the baby. When they told us we were having a boy, as a mother of two daughters, it really softened my mom's heart toward it all. It was as if the doctor told her she was the one having the boy.

When I was still two months away from my due date, one night my mother and I were watching *The Original Kings of Comedy*. I was laughing so hard that I started to get contractions. I couldn't believe it—I was going into labor. My mother rushed me off to the hospital. After hours of labor, our son Andre Jr. was born, with my mother by my side the whole time.

Tiffiney

Unfortunately, I was not with Tiff when our son Andre Jr. (we call him Poppy) was born. I wanted to be there, but I didn't have the resources to sit in Seattle and wait for his birth. I was in North Oakland when I got the call from Tiff that she had gone into labor. I felt helpless.

My head was all over the place, with different emotions bouncing around—fear, excitement, guilt for not being there. I was trying to get frequent updates on the phone from her mother. "How's she doing?"

I paced around the apartment complex, trying to burn energy, distract myself. I walked up and down the long flight of stairs outside the apartment and back and forth on the long walkway in front of the door. I was so nervous.

When I finally got word from Remel that Andre Jr. had arrived, it felt surreal. I sat down and stared off in a daze, trying to collect my thoughts. Reality hit me really hard: *Man, I'm a dad.* I felt proud, like I had stepped into manhood, but scared to death at the same time. I was young, but I already had a lot of responsibility. Would I be able to handle this? I now had my own family that I needed to care for. It was time to man up.

I went to school the next day and told my close friends that Tiffiney finally had the baby. Everybody was shocked. "Bro, that's crazy, are you serious?" *As a heart attack*, I said. I heard that more than once, the reactions you would expect from high school kids. While a lot of them were telling me, "It's gonna be alright," I was thinking, *I don't know if it's gonna be alright.* But what else were they supposed to say?

I made it to Washington a few weeks later. He had been two months premature, but by the time I got there he was out of the NICU and at home. When I held him for the first time, swaddled in blankets, I was in awe. *This is crazy. This is my son.* My shock was combined with a conviction that I needed to get my life together. Unfortunately, it would take another year and a half for that conviction to come to fruition. But Poppy's birth was the beginning of that journey.

I was so impressed by Tiffiney's maturity after the birth. That's something I love about her—I didn't see her blink. Of course, she had moments when she broke down because of everything she was dealing with, the baby and the ongoing conflicts with her mom. She was on government assistance, getting WIC to help stay afloat. She always had this fight in her, a sense of fearlessness. She was only sixteen, now with a reputation, but she was never ashamed of our child or ashamed of her relationship with me. She stood strong and shouldered it all. She's always been a soldier. She went to night school at a local college to make up for lost credits and eventually walked the stage at her high school graduation with a baby on her hip. That's the type of girl I was dating. She was different. I was the man in the situation, so I felt a pressure to take care of them, but she was dealing with a lot more than I was dealing with. She was the one who was taking care of a newborn baby, a twenty-four seven responsibility. And she wasn't the type to pass the baby off to her mom and dip out.

When Poppy was a few months old, they came down to California to visit. My dad immediately fell in love with the baby. He got over the shock, anger, and frustration and just embraced our situation. He called little Dre "The Boss"; he said Dre was a fat baby who loved to eat. His attitude was, *Okay, we have to help support this girl.* He also fell in love with Tiffiney right away. He called her his daughter and loved her as if she were his own. If my dad had an affinity for you, you were going to feel it. He loved big. When he saw her, he hugged and kissed her. He was very affectionate.

I can't say that my mother felt the same about Tiffiney. I could tell when she looked at Tiffiney she was thinking, *Who is this woman who trapped my son?* She was skeptical. My aunties were skeptical too. They all went through the pleasantries and said the right things, but I knew they felt a way about Tiffiney. In their minds, I was supposed to make it and then some girl trapped me. Though they probably wouldn't admit it, the women in the family looked at her sideways.

Just after I turned seventeen, I won the U.S. National Championships and started bringing in some money from USA Boxing. I was the number one fighter in the United States at 165 pounds. That $1,500 a month was right on time, as I was trying to see Tiff and the baby as often as possible and contribute to the costs of raising a newborn.

Around this time, my mother had spiraled into addiction again. I would be receiving phone calls from some of the people from our neighborhood, telling me my mother had gotten into a fight with this person or that person. When I talked to her on the phone, she told on herself every time, especially if she was drunk or high. She couldn't hide it.

At this point, I had completely stopped going to school. Academics were not a main priority. I was staying anywhere I could rest my head. My home base was Jonathan's grandmother's house in Washington. It wasn't quite a trap house, but there was always a lot of shady stuff going on there. Honestly, I was contributing to some of the shadiness. On any given day, I would be out with some of my dudes, hitting licks—to keep money in our pockets, I would steal drugs from the local drug dealers. We would meet up, and I would survey what they brought and simply strong-arm them and dare them to do something about it. I was reckless, I know, and my actions could have cost me my life. I would get threats from this one and that one: "If I catch him, I'm going to kill him." I took the threats serious because I knew I was doing wrong. I tried to stay out of the way of as much as I could, but trouble felt like it inevitably found me.

I was in one of my stints where it was all about the streets, and I wasn't thinking about boxing. My first thought waking up was, *What am I getting into today—what's the next move?* I was looking for profit and pleasure. There were brief moments where I found myself missing the sport, and even missing the grind, but not enough for me to stop what I was doing. Even though I had slipped far from my foundation in God, I still felt him and knew he was a genuine prayer away. My conscience would accuse me at times when I did wrong, but I became a master at suppressing those thoughts and feelings. I started to believe the lies I was telling myself, that I wasn't too bad and I'd get myself together when I was ready. I was deceived. The coldest part about self-deception is the deceived party doesn't know they are deceived and continues as if everything is alright. It took years, but when my eyes were open, I began to understand how arrogant, selfish, and reckless I had been. That I was squandering the gifts and talents I had been given. I was one bad decision away from crashing out and blowing it all. I'm fully convinced that what should have happened to me didn't come to pass because someone was praying. That's God's mercy.

I kept getting warnings, people who God was sending to me. Virg would call me on occasion. I knew he probably was exercising a lot of restraint because Millie was on him constantly—"You gotta go get Dre! You gotta do something!"

Whether I was in Oakland or Seattle, people who saw me would report back to him. "I saw Dre, man. He seems like he's full-blown out there. Dre don't look good."

Virg would tell them, "Yeah, I'm praying for him, man. He's gonna be alright. He might have to learn the hard way."

He wasn't chasing me down every day. He was praying and trusting God. When he felt compelled, he would call me and give me a few words. I know he felt my time of grace was running out, and I was starting to feel that way too.

"God is not gonna let you get away with nothing, brotha. He's got his hand on you," he would warn me. "We are two years out from the Olympics. Dre, remember we used to count down the years? Well, it's around the corner. We're two years out, man. It's time for you to come home and get focused."

Sometimes his warnings would frustrate me, and I would get mad. Other times, I was thankful he called, because I knew he was right. "I know, V. I hear you. I appreciate you calling."

I tried to remain respectful, but I wasn't trying to hear it. When people were calling Virg and reporting my missteps, they were thinking about the boxing only. What I appreciated about Virg is that he was thinking far beyond the boxing.

"I'm not worried about Andre the boxer," he told people. "I'm worried about Andre the man. If I can just get the man right, the boxing is going to take care of itself."

God was using Virg to be a voice in my life, a source of warning and encouragement when I needed it the most. But warnings were not just coming from Virg. One night I was sitting in a parked car in front of my grandmother's house smoking weed when my phone rang. It was my mother. She was clean at the time and doing good.

"What's up, Mom?"

"Dre, baby, I don't know what you're doing, but you need to stop," she said.

"Ma, I ain't doing nothin'. Maybe smoking a little weed. That's it." Ironically that's the same thing she used to tell me.

"I don't know, Dre," she said. "I'm just telling you what I feel in my spirit and what I feel deep in my heart. You need to stop whatever you're doing."

In the past, I would be the voice of reason for my mother, and now she was that voice for me. My mother continued to warn me, and she never stopped praying.

When I hung up, I was genuinely concerned. That one made me stop and think. *What are you doing with your life? What if your time is running out? You're getting all these warnings for a reason.* I sat still and thought deeply about my mother's words. I knew she was right, but I wasn't ready to hear them. I was doing me, living the life I wanted to live. Selfishly, I shook off her words, suppressed another warning—and reached for the blunt. I may have toned it down a bit that night, but the next day I was back on my run.

I would go into stores and steal bottles of alcohol, like Moët. Whatever we didn't drink, we would sell. I was a hustler; I never was fully broke. People started calling us the Moët Boys. When I was ready to make a move, I would always have on a peacoat, even if it was hot outside; an XXXL white tee; some over-oversized Girbaud jeans; and some Jordans. I'd walk down the alcohol aisle and slip the bottle of Moët in the center of my pants. My waist size was probably a 30 or 32, but these pants would be 36 or 38, to give me more room to work. Another two bottles would go in my sleeves. I convinced myself that I didn't look hot or suspicious, but I lied to myself. I think employees knew; they just didn't care enough to do anything. When we got back to the house, we'd sometimes put ecstasy pills in the Moët bottle and drink the bubbling concoction. We were reckless and just living from moment to moment.

One night, I had been partying, and on the way home, I stopped at one of the usual stores I would hit. I was already lit and moving sloppy. I really don't know why I was there, because I certainly didn't need any more alcohol. I went down my usual aisle, but because I was already intoxicated, I didn't even try to hide the bottles. With the bottles in my hand, I began to walk out the front door.

But there was a store employee who was trying to be a hero. He placed himself in front of me, locked the door, and said, "You're not leaving."

"Bro, get out of my way," I said.

"You're not leaving with those bottles," he said.

I thank God I didn't do anything to that employee that night. I could have put my hands on him and drastically changed my life forever. My life would look a lot different. I put the bottles down just long enough to unlock the door myself.

"Man, I'm taking these bottles—move!" He finally moved out of my way.

I climbed back into the car and we headed to Grandma Barb's house.

It didn't take long for me to pass out on the couch. I woke up to loud noises and shouting. When I opened my eyes, there were guns and tasers pointed at me. They had raided the party at the house—there was always a party going on at that house. From the way the cops were acting, you would have thought I robbed a bank. Everybody that was in the house had left. That's typically how it goes when things get real. You are standing there alone, forced to shoulder the consequences of your actions by yourself.

"What?" I said, confused. I climbed off the couch and showed them my hands. They cuffed me and shoved me in the back of a police cruiser. One of the officers turned to me before he walked away.

"You got anything to say for yourself?" he said.

I verbalized the one thought that kept coming back to me. "I just want to go back home," I said. "I need to get back to Oakland."

They brought me to the county jail; I appeared in court about thirty-six hours later. They were trying to charge me with all kinds of crazy offenses, like strong-arm robbery and other things that sounded over the top. Behind the scenes, Virg was working furiously on my behalf. His day job was as a probation officer, so he started calling the DA's office in Washington, telling them I was his godson. He worked something out where he would come pick me up, I'd be released to him and Millie, and I would be placed on probation, with the promise to stay out of trouble. All of my accomplishments as a boxer, and the fact that I was an Olympic hopeful, were working for me.

When I called Virg from the county jail and he told me what he had done, I was upset.

"Man, why would you do that? What do you mean, you got to come get me? I'm a grown man, I ain't no kid."

"Dre, you don't even know what you're saying," he countered. "This could save your life. I sat back and I waited. I waited and now God is telling me to move. It's time to move."

I was disgusted, and I am not completely sure why. Maybe I saw it as another form of control—the kind of control I had been trying to escape. I didn't think I needed any help from him, or anybody else. The next day when I walked out of that jail, I heard the birds chirping; the sun was shining bright. It had only been thirty-six hours, but it felt like six years. Millie, who had made the trip to pick me up, brought me to Grandma Barb's house to get my stuff.

"I'm going to give you a couple of hours and then I'm coming back so we can leave," she said.

Tiffiney came over to see me; I told her how upset I was about them controlling my movements.

"You're the main reason I come up here," I told her. "I need to be able to move the way I want to move."

I looked at her and made a promise. "I'm gonna come back and get you," I said solemnly.

I didn't have any resources or money, so I had no idea how I was going to make good on that promise. I wasn't in a good place with boxing. My life was in shambles. But in my spirit, I knew she and the baby needed to be with me.

When I got back to California, I had a conversation with Virg about my future.

"You need to put all the foolishness down," he said. "You're gonna blow it, son. God's got this for you. We've been planning to win a gold medal your whole life. We are less than two years out. Dre, you got just enough time to go and qualify."

I told him I needed Tiffiney to be with me.

"Do you love her? Can you see yourself marrying her?" Virg asked. I said, "Yes."

"Well, we'll find a way for her to get down here if that's what you need to stay on track." That commitment from Virg stopped me from going back up to Washington and allowed me to turn my life around.

I was now pregnant again, and Dre intently explained to me his dreams of going to the Olympics, becoming a world champion in boxing and changing our lives forever. I don't know if it was the look in his eye or the confidence in his voice but I believed every word. About two weeks later Andre was calling me asking me to come and live with him in Oakland.

Next thing I knew, I was telling my mom that I was moving to California to be with Andre after I graduated. I knew this was a huge step, but I also knew I wasn't crazy. We loved each other and we wanted to be together. It was that simple.

When I moved to California, I was blown away by how supportive Millie and Virgil were. From day one, Virg treated me like a daughter. We had our own little bedroom downstairs in the basement, where we stayed with the baby. When Andre and I had our first big argument, I was curious to see how Virg and Millie would react.

But they surprised me. Virg pulled me to the side, sat me down, and started talking to me about what it means to be a wife and partner, what it looks like from a biblical standpoint. And what it looks like for Andre to be a husband. Most of the time when we had disagreements, Virg would have my back—to the point where Dre sometimes would get angry.

"Why are you always on her side, Virg?" Andre would voice.

They poured so much into our relationship. In the early stages, they were encouraging us to get married.

"Listen, I've made some mistakes," Virg told us. "You guys do better, because I know you *can* do better."

Tiffiney

EIGHT

MY FATHER'S HEART

I was only ten years old when I had my first fight. I was a child prodigy who gave up a childhood for the sport. Within boxing circles, they began to say, "Oh, he's the one"—and I wasn't even out of elementary school yet. That was my life. By the time I got into my late teens, I didn't want my life to be on the clock anymore. I wanted freedom from the rigid schedule. I didn't want to be worried about keeping my weight down for upcoming fights and tournaments. But I didn't have the courage to say I was burned out, or even the capacity to know myself. Other people's identities—my dad's, Virgil's—were wrapped up in my success. There had been a significant financial investment in me. I was aware of all of that, making it even harder for me to say something. So I took the path that was easier for me: I ran away from the sport. I dove into drugs. I embraced partying, trying to numb myself.

I was battling depression, but I didn't acknowledge it at the time. I learned later that depression and anxiety run heavy on my father's side of the family; I saw my dad struggle with those two giants while

I was growing up. Aunts and uncles too. Apparently, I got unhealthy doses of both. At one point when I was about seventeen, my father encouraged me to start taking an antidepressant called Paxil. He gave me a few little sample boxes of the pills. When Tiff saw the pills, she told me, "Dre, don't take that."

"My dad says I should take it," I said.

"I respect your dad, but don't take that."

She took the samples and stashed them away in a cabinet. I would see them sitting there when I went into the cabinet, but I never touched them. In hindsight, I'm so glad I had Tiffiney around me to intervene. She didn't want me to become dependent on the medication for the next twenty or thirty years if there was any way to avoid it. I'm not here to judge those who take antidepressants. Everyone should do what works best for them. I just don't think it was for me. By the grace of God, I gained knowledge on how to fight when I feel gripped with fear and anxiety. In the church, I also gained a lot of deliverance from the hold of these generational demons that were controlling a large part of life for me.

As I tried to run away from boxing, God was steadily trying to get my attention, letting life hit me upside the head. I couldn't get away with anything. I could be surrounded by ten people and the police would "randomly" pick me out of the crowd for questioning.

I managed to clean myself up in the weeks leading up to the Under-19 National Championships in Reno, Nevada, in 2002, the biggest national tournament for seventeen- and eighteen-year-old boxers. Working with Virg, I was in pretty good shape. When we got to the Eldorado Casino in Reno, I saw the draw; I would be fighting my rival Curtis Stevens in the first round. Curtis would be looking for revenge after I beat him years ago in the National Silver Gloves when we were ten, the last time we had fought.

"Dad, I'm fighting Curtis in the first round of the tournament," I told my father over the phone. He was still in California for work. He was now on staff at New Bridge, the rehab program he had gone through to get clean.

"I'm gonna find a way to get off," he said. "I'll call you back."

He picked up Tiffiney and drove the five hours from the Bay Area to Reno, both of them sweating the whole way in the dead of summer in his Honda CRX two-seater with no A/C—Tiff carrying our second child in her belly. I was so glad they made the trip; I especially needed my dad in that building. His presence alone gave me confidence. My mother was also there; she didn't come to many of my fights. I was able to capture a rare picture of the two of them in Reno, with me in the middle, cheesing—the way it was always supposed to be.

Uncle Bob, who also made the trip to Reno, sat with my dad in the casino during the tournament and listened while Dad expressed his worry about some of the promoters and managers who had started to sniff around me at this point. Since I was one of the top amateur fighters in the country, I had drawn the interest of many business types in the boxing world looking to attach themselves to me before I turned professional. I was walking around with a big dollar sign on my back; that idea made my pops profoundly uncomfortable. My dad and Bob were boxing historians—they devoured *The Ring* and *Boxing Illustrated* every month; they knew all the unsavory characters who leeched from boxers through the generations and left them penniless. My father, who had run a successful business before the drugs took him down, was astute when it came to business practices, and he always had great instincts and street smarts. He could read a person as they walked in a room. I feel like I got that gift from him too. His worries sometimes caused tension between him and Virgil because he felt like Virgil wasn't consulting him enough.

Watching my dad, Uncle Bob sensed he wasn't completely himself. At times he seemed a bit confused, like he was in a fog. He then confessed to Bob that he had driven himself to the hospital in Reno because he was having chest pains. Apparently, they determined he wasn't in any danger, so they released him. His weight had ballooned; he was probably fifty or sixty pounds overweight. Uncle Bob was concerned about what was going on with him, but he didn't say anything to me about it. When I look back at the picture we took with my mom, I can see that my dad clearly was not well. But I didn't notice it at the time.

After I beat Curtis and went on to win the Under-19 National Championships, we were all in high spirits when I returned to the Bay Area. Tiffiney now saw how realistic the dream was that I had planned for us. She realized that I was the best fighter in the country and that maybe I would win a gold medal, become a world champion, and make good on the promises I made to her.

I took off from training for a week after the tournament to rest my body. My dad would typically pick me up in the morning at Virg and Millie's in East Oakland to take me running. It was an important way for him to feel involved and connected to my training. But when I was ready to start up again, he called me on Monday morning and canceled.

"I don't feel too good," he said. "I think I have the flu or something. Do you mind if I don't pick you up?"

"Yeah, sure, it's all good, Dad," I said. "Don't trip."

Those were the last words I ever said to my father.

The next morning, I got a call from my cousin Debbie—the daughter of his sister Sandy. Her voice sounded crazy when I picked up.

"Dre, he's gone!" she said hysterically.

"What are you talking about?"

"Your dad is dead! He had a heart attack. He's gone."

I felt a numbness spread over my entire body. I couldn't believe what I was hearing. *A heart attack? But how?*

I went upstairs to find Virg. I told Tiffiney to hold the phone. I was strangely calm, walking like I was in a trance.

"My dad died," I told them.

"What are you talking about?" Virg said.

"Debbie just called me. They took him to Eden Medical Center. But she said he's gone."

I don't remember much as we drove to the hospital; everything was a blur. I was moving but not feeling, almost like I was holding my breath the whole time. In the emergency room waiting area, we got the news that he had died in the ambulance on the way to the hospital. I learned that he had heart disease so bad that he should have been on a list to get a transplant.

They let me go into the room where his body was being kept, some kind of hospital morgue where they stored the dead. His was the only body in the room. He was on a cold-slab table, partially covered with a sheet. Superman was gone. I walked toward him slowly, trying to hold it together. I reached out and touched his hand. It was ice cold. I felt the finality of that reality crashing down on me, flooding my senses. He was both my dad and my mom for much of my life, the person who had absolute dominion over my world, determining the quality of my existence. If I had food in my mouth, clothes on my back, a place to lay my head, it was because of Duke Ward. I leaned over and situated my mouth near his left ear. I knew his soul was gone, but I still felt compelled to deliver a final message.

"I'm gonna finish what we started," I whispered.

I was talking about everything. Finishing school. Becoming the man he raised me to be. Winning the Olympic gold medal and becoming a world champion.

A few months after my father died, we had a bright light of happiness push aside the gloom, at least for a while, when Tiff gave birth to our son Malachi. He was born at Summit Medical Center in Oakland, this time two weeks early. Tiffiney and I were eighteen years old, with two kids, living in one room in the basement of a house of two people who weren't our parents but had become family.

Although I had many reasons to bathe in the joy of my growing and loving family, I couldn't shake the deep depression that had taken hold of me when I lost my dad. I turned again to the escape I had come to rely on—drugs and alcohol.

I was working odd jobs to get money, at one point scrubbing cars at a car wash. We had Tiffiney's public assistance money from the government, and we had my stipend from USA Boxing. But my head wasn't right.

I'm not sure if my drug use reached the level of addiction, but I was comfortable using, numbing, and escaping my responsibilities. I had to find a way to get refocused. A big part of that was trying to recapture my faith.

My mother was clean and started coming back into the picture. She had been attending a church in Richmond, California, called God's Way, and she invited us to come with her. It was about a forty-five-minute drive for us, but we were willing to do it. We felt like we needed more stability and a foundation under us as we were raising a young family. We rededicated our lives to God at that church. We started driving out there a couple days a week, really making that commitment for each other and for our kids. God used my mother as an instrument to get me and my wife back into the church to help us rededicate our lives to God. If we had stayed on the path we were on, we wouldn't have made it as a couple and we probably would have ruined our lives.

There's a scripture in 1 Corinthians that speaks to this season in my life. It says, "One plants, one waters, and God gives the increase" (3:6, my paraphrase). I had people around me planting and watering seeds—Tiffiney, my mom, my sister, Virg. My faith was being revived. God was giving the increase, little by little. I was still struggling, but the hardness in my heart was being broken up. When I started to give God my will, he gradually began to take the taste for drugs and alcohol out of my mouth. God met me where I was. He was always there, but until then I wasn't willing. I couldn't access His power. I could no longer feel His presence when I was running in rebellion. But when I began to feel God again, to sense him, I knew I had to rededicate myself. The Olympics were now a year and a half away—I had to get this right.

I was going to service more frequently, and I felt God drawing me closer to him. I would find myself at the front of the church whenever there was an altar call. I felt like there was an invisible force pulling me to the front. I would cry and sob as I lay on my face. I didn't care who was watching; I was fighting for my life. I needed God. All I could think about was how over the last few years I had made my bed in hell but he never left me. My change and conversion weren't instant. I still smoked at times—but it didn't have the same impact. After a while, I would flush whatever I had left down the toilet. Finally, I got to the point where I put it down and didn't pick it back up and never picked it back up. Through God, I experienced true and total deliverance. The majority of this transformation took place at a new church we started attending, The Well Christian Community, led by Pastor Napoleon Kaufman.

The depression started to lift and I began to feel happy and joyous again. This was the main thing that attracted me to Christianity: the power that I experienced. If the Bible were just a book of old writings and rules, I wouldn't have found solace. It was the tangible power that I experienced, along with the love of God, that won me over. I needed a Savior, not just a book full of principles. I started to open my Bible and feel God speaking to me through the Scriptures. That was powerful! As the heaviness began to lift and my mind became clearer, I started to think different, feel different. I *was* different. I was becoming a new person, and it was evident to those around me. I was hungry for God.

Tiff and I began to heal as well. We embraced each other and really learned what it meant to be married from a biblical view. We were babies with babies, but I never stopped believing we could make it, as long as we didn't give up. It wasn't easy, but my theory proved to be true. We knew the next step was for us to get married, to complete the circle.

On April 8, 2003, we officially joined together as one. I was nineteen; Tiff was eighteen. We had two kids. I was scared to death, but we now had God, and we had an abundance of young love. And we had hope.

NINE

OLYMPIC GLORY

I got fully locked in on boxing just in time for the Olympic qualifiers. Earning the title of Olympian is not an easy process. After winning the Olympic Trials and the Box-Offs the following week, I had to face the best boxers in North, Central, and South America. The team headed south to Tijuana, Mexico, for the American Olympic Qualifier in March of 2004, where I officially earned a light heavyweight berth in the 2004 Olympic Games. As soon as I clinched my spot on the Olympic team, I became the official property of USA Boxing. They made me work for that monthly check. USA Boxing had several stipulations for being on the team; the most crucial was that I now had a new boxing coach. For the first time in my career, I had a voice in my ear that didn't belong to Virgil Hunter. But I was blessed to have a guy named Basheer Abdullah coaching the Olympic team. He had been the head coach for the Army boxing team for fifteen years and had watched me fight at the Nationals throughout the years. He had even coached against me as I fought a few of his guys in the past. Coach

Abdullah didn't come in with a lot of ego, which was a rarity among amateur-boxing coaches. I owe him a great deal because he understood right away what I needed, which was to stay close to the man who had trained me my whole life, and to watch me closely so that I would not overdo it and overtrain.

"Dre, you're a special kid, and I'm honored to coach you," Coach Abdullah told me. "I have to stay in contact with Virg as often as I can to make sure you are training properly and that my coaching is in line with what he has been teaching you."

I was surprised and excited to hear that from Coach Abdullah. All I had ever heard was how the Olympic coach was going to try to squeeze my main coach out of the picture and try to change my boxing style to fit his style of teaching. Those were the experiences that many amateur fighters had encountered through the years, but Coach Abdullah put that idea to rest right away for me. I was relieved.

I was a fighter who needed monitoring in my overall training. I was young and had not experienced a loss in boxing since I was fourteen years old. I feel as though there were times that my winning streak worked for me and sometimes against me. It worked for me in the sense that I hated losing and it fostered my drive to keep winning. I never cheated in training; I never cut corners; I was afraid to. But the streak probably worked against me at times because that drive, coupled with a fear of losing, drove me to a place where I would always overdo it. This left me in constant danger of overtraining. Nobody outworked me at the Olympic Training Center before we went to Athens, Greece, for the 2004 Olympics. On our morning runs, I finished in first place about 95 percent of the time. My teammate Andre Dirrell would keep up and battle me for first place on our runs on any given day. I was the first guy to arrive at the boxing gym for training and the last guy to leave. Basheer was always keeping a close watch on me, closer than I even knew at the time. He would see me training later than the other guys, my body weight would start to drop, and he would start to get worried, so he would call Virg.

"Look, don't let him run every day with the team," Virg told him. "Dre runs hard—he's not just jogging. Make him run every other day. He needs to rest as much as possible. Basheer, he's gonna want to do extra training after the workout. Pick the day that he can do it, but don't let him do it every day."

I couldn't help it; that's just who I was and how I had been raised. I had been dreaming about the Olympics since I was ten. The plan was always to win a gold medal. I couldn't even conceive how I'd feel if I fell short of the gold. We never talked about anything but gold; it was a foregone conclusion in our minds. Not in an arrogant way, but we believed it was destined. I knew it wasn't going to be easy. I knew I was going to be undersized. And I had never fought a Russian before; I had never fought a Cuban. Those were the guys who were dominating the international boxing world at that time.

Admittedly, part of that was by design. Virg decided that it was better for me if the other countries never got a chance to fight me before we met in Athens, so he told USA Boxing that I couldn't always participate when they tried to get me to some of the international tournaments in the lead-up to Athens. I only had a handful of international fights under my belt, and none at the highest level, like the world championships or the Pan American Games. Virg wouldn't let me go and they would always get mad at him. He would tell them, "If he goes, all you're doing is giving them some tape on him for the opposing coach to come up with a game plan to beat Andre."

Virg knew the other countries wouldn't take me seriously anyway because I was small. I was spotting many of their fighters eight or nine pounds and two or three inches in height. I really should have been fighting in the 165-pound division, one weight class below where I actually was fighting at 178 pounds. The full Olympic qualifying process takes about a year. Virg thought I was going to have another growth spurt within that time frame and felt my body needed the extra space to grow. He overcalculated; my body stayed the same, and I remained a 165-pound fighter, fighting thirteen pounds north of where I should have been fighting. I guess things don't always work out according to plan, or maybe they do. Virg knew that by the time they realized how good I was, it was going to be too late and the fight would be over.

In the U.S., observers thought I would do okay, not great. ESPN published an article predicting the medal count for boxing and had me winning the bronze. The fighters and coaches who knew me from watching me fight over the years generally felt like I had a real shot at a gold medal. Internationally, I was on nobody's radar, and rightfully so.

By 2004, Olympic boxing in the U.S. had fallen far from its glory days, when the boxing matches were aired on prime-time television with guys like Sugar Ray Leonard. Leonard became a household name from winning Olympic gold in 1976. People all over the world had learned about Sugar Ray's story before he had his first professional fight. In addition, we were now wearing headgear in the Olympics, so viewers couldn't really see our faces like they could in previous years, which also lessened the likelihood that the public would recognize and become enamored with us. U.S. Olympic boxing also suffered a public relations blow when Ricardo Williams, the 2000 Olympic light welterweight silver medalist—and probably one of the best amateurs who's ever lived, in my eyes—was arrested on drug charges with intent to distribute just before the 2004 Olympics began. Williams and Rocky Juarez, who also won a silver, were the top medalists on the U.S. team in 2000. Williams, who got a huge $1.4 million signing bonus when he turned pro, and a lot more money when he had his first professional fight on HBO, was the biggest star on the U.S. Olympic boxing team. But when Ricardo turned pro, the streets came calling, and Rick couldn't walk away.

At that time, if you wanted to watch Olympic boxing in the United States, you would have to tune in to CNBC or MSNBC at two or three in the morning. The network airing the Olympics decided boxing was no longer a priority, nor deserving of a prime-time slot. I wouldn't understand the implications of this until later into my professional career. At the time I didn't care about where my fight was being shown or if it was being shown at all. All I cared about was gold.

When it was time to leave for Athens, I decided that I would go alone—Tiffiney wasn't going to come with me. She was not happy. I think she still might be working through her forgiveness process on that matter to this day. But 2004 was a very ugly time on the world stage, especially for the United States of America. We had gone to war the year before; things were very volatile. The United States was not well liked outside our borders. We felt it constantly when we were in Athens—whenever they announced anyone from the U.S., there would be a loud chorus of boos. They saw us as bullies; they saw us as spoiled. They hated us. I knew that was the climate even before I got there. I was hearing about a strong possibility of a terrorist attack, bombings, all kinds of stuff. I told Tiff, "I want you to come, but we can't risk it. You have to stay home." She fought real hard on that. She was hurt and angry, but I felt like I was doing the right thing. I told all my family members the same thing, that the environment might not be safe, but a few didn't listen to me. My aunt Sue, uncle Joe, and a couple of my cousins made the trip. When I saw them in the crowd with homemade signs, cheering for me, I was glad they didn't listen to me and came anyway. Virg also made his way there and his presence in Athens made a difference for me even though Olympic regulations didn't allow him to be in my corner. I didn't realize that I needed some familiar faces in the crowd until I was there.

In addition to the safety issue, Virg thought family would be another distraction that I did not need. "Dre, a lot of these guys have family members here," Virg told me. "And when they should be resting, they are going to be wasting a lot of energy walking around, sightseeing. This is not a vacation. We are here on a mission; we need to finish what we started. If you sacrifice your comfort for the next two weeks, your life will change forever."

So once again, I was in a whole different mindset than most of the dudes around me. I watched my teammates interacting with their families, worrying about whether they got in safely, where they were staying, at which gate they're going to meet in order to get them into the Olympic Village. Some of my teammates would stay out with their families for hours on their off days. I didn't have any of that. I felt lonely; I didn't have my family present, nor did I have a lot of comfort, but in reality, I was used to this. I spent a lot of alone time with God, reading my Bible, praying. I was facing giants that were bigger than me, fear and doubt. Fighting for my belief that I was in Athens, Greece, with purpose—for a time such as this—caused my faith to grow. I was utterly dependent on God to get me through. I am a firm believer that faith without works is dead (James 2:17). I knew I had taken care of my responsibilities, training and focusing on what was before me, but this was beyond what I could accomplish in my own strength. I needed God to continue to encourage me and ultimately empower me to run to the battle during insurmountable odds. God did just that.

I had a lifeline to Virg: a prepaid phone. We would talk daily; his voice and words kept me levelheaded and full of faith. We talked strategy at times, but mainly he would be working on my mind. "God has you here for a purpose; this is all a part of the plan. Don't worry about being undersized; you are strong enough. These guys can't beat you."

That's what I needed—some faith talk. And a little reassurance that I belonged at this level, and not only did I belong, but that I was destined to win.

Staying connected to Virg and having Coach Abdullah were two big pieces of the puzzle for my success in Athens. I had a few other key figures I heavily relied upon too. One was a veteran trainer from Philly, Al Mitchell, who ran an Olympic boxing program at Northern Michigan University. Al was the team's technical advisor, but for me he was so much more. Me and Al would spend time together talking boxing and listening to oldies while he drank his tea. I have and always will have deep respect for the older generation. I needed Al; he had already made a successful Olympic run as head coach of the '96 Olympic team in Atlanta. David Reid was America's only boxing gold medalist in those Games; Reid was Al's fighter, and that brought me comfort knowing Al Mitchell had already fought and won a battle that I was now engaging in. He and I would slip away to the American College of Greece to watch film of my upcoming opponents. We both were avid students of the sport, so this was a perfect fit. I was surprised that no one else was interested in watching tape. Most of us were young and felt like winning was a foregone conclusion, but it wasn't going to be that easy. While most of the time we could get by with that mentality in the States, I'm not sure everyone understood that we were about to face an entirely different beast. The Russians and Cubans were basically professionals—full-time fighters who were supported by their countries to do nothing other than win. The Cubans trained at a place called The Farm. Promising kids got pulled from their homes at a young age and sent to The Farm, which was extremely regimented. All they did was train, fight, and prepare for the big stage, the Olympic

Games. There are levels to preparation—the Cubans and the Russians were on a very different plane than the Americans when it came to prepping fighters. We *wanted* to win; the Cubans and Russians *needed* to win for a better quality of life. That was the mentality we were going to be facing.

The other person who proved to be a godsend for me was a strength-and-conditioning coach and physical therapist named Don Chu. I had worked with him in California since I was thirteen. He was in Athens as a physical therapist for the U.S. synchronized swimming team. I knew he was going to be there, and we would frequently meet up. Don was instrumental in helping me recover from fight to fight, deal with any nagging injuries, and help my body get to the finish line.

Athens is where I was first introduced to the benefits of ice baths. My body was so tired and broken up between fights because I was facing much bigger guys. I knew I needed some way to recover quickly to help me bounce back for my next fight. When I asked around, I was told to try the ice bath. The only athletes I saw in the cold tubs were track athletes. They would only go into the cold bath from their waist down. My whole body was wrecked, so I submerged myself in the tub from my neck down, for twenty minutes at a time. I was desperate. My body hurt. I needed to recover fast, as I had another beast waiting for me in my next fight. I was under no illusions; many of the fighters from the other countries despised us. Their attitude was, *If we don't beat anybody else, we are gonna beat you Americans.* You felt it and you saw it in their faces.

When we got the draw and I saw that I would not be fighting on the first night of the Olympics, I was relieved. That meant I could attend the opening ceremonies to officially kick off the 2004 Olympic Games. This still ranks as one of the greatest experiences of my life. As I walked into that stadium, surrounded by all the athletes from around the globe, it finally hit me: *I'm at the Olympics!* This was different. I could actually feel the goosebumps forming on my arms as I sported the outfit they gave Team USA members in our care packages.

I saw the track stars, like Allyson Felix and Justin Gatlin.

As I walked around the stadium, I felt like I could sense my father's presence. The event was enormous to me. It was something I had dreamed about for so long—I was finally there, on the world's stage. With my father on my mind and in my heart, I was there with *one* purpose: win gold.

At the bus stop in the Olympic Village, a guy walked up to me out of nowhere, a guy I'd never seen in my life, and said, "God has you here for a reason." Then he walked off. I was shocked. Little did this person know that what he said to me was exactly what I needed to hear in that moment. There is a passage in the Bible that reads, "A word spoken in due season, how good it is!" (Proverbs 15:23). That moment was not only good and timely, but it was another little sign that served as a reminder that while the moment was big, it wasn't too big for me, and that God was with me every step of the way.

As I processed where I was and what I was there to do, God led me to the story of David and Goliath in the book of 1 Samuel. It was my first time reading the whole story word for word; the words felt so real to me, the revelation so strong, it lifted off the pages for me. I came into the Olympics at 170 pounds, but light heavyweights in Europe were a lot bigger than me—dudes who were dropping down to 178 from 200 pounds or even more. They were taller, too—six foot two or six foot three to my six feet. When I went to my first weigh-in, I felt a little insecure about my size. It's funny how no matter how confident you think you are, fears and insecurities will still rise up. All of this was Virg's plan, but I knew my natural weight was more like 165 pounds, with the middleweights. I ate two PowerBars and drank Gatorade on the morning bus ride to the weigh-ins, doing whatever I could to put more weight on. I wanted to look like I belonged at the weight class. Those few PowerBars and Gatorades would move the scale slightly north, but they weren't going to do anything for my stature. In my mind I guess I felt bigger—until I stepped on the scale and the weighmaster looked at me and laughed.

"Oh, you're little!" he said. "You're small!"

I nodded my head as if to say, *Just wait and see.* On the international stage they do weight in kilograms, but in pounds the scale said I was 170.5. Man, I thought I would at least be 172 pounds. I truly felt like I was David, about to face the Goliaths of the light heavyweight class. In the book of 1 Samuel, when David approached Goliath, doubt swirled around him. The men from Israel were battle-tested, but they were scared of Goliath, towering over them at well over nine feet tall. Goliath was taunting them, mocking Israel and their God. The Israelites were so terrified of this giant Philistine that they did nothing. If we allow it, fear has a way of paralyzing us and can cause us to forget who we are and what we have come to do. I had to overcome fear first if I was going to win. I was David, going up against all these Olympic giants. This was it—the scripture was coming to life.

When we got the draw to finally see who we were going to face in our brackets, some grumbled about how tough my draw was. I had the Cuban Yoan Pablo Hernández in my bracket; I had the Russian Evgeny Makarenko, who had been a dominant two-time world champion in the light heavyweight division for several years, and the favorite to win the gold; and I had Utkirbek Haydarov from Uzbekistan, who had won a world championship as a middleweight.

Virg heard about all the pessimism and grumbling, but he wasn't going to hear it from me. "What are you complaining about? This is the way it's supposed to be," he said. "I wouldn't expect it to be any other way. You think you're gonna get to this point and have it easy? You're supposed to mow through every single one of these dudes."

Virg is crazy, I thought. But he wasn't, he was just full of faith. Faith is contagious; what was on Virg continued to rub off on me. The stage was set—the moment for my first fight at the Olympic Games was here.

TEN

OLYMPIC GOLD AND THE BUSINESS OF BOXING

When I walked out for my first fight, I was so nervous. I was facing Clemente Russo of Italy, who was about the same height as me but had a much thicker build. I stepped in the ring and felt my legs shaking so much that I bounced up and down on my toes so Russo couldn't see them shake. This was the culmination of everything I had trained for over the course of more than a decade. All the sacrifices, all the ups and downs, all led to this moment. Virg had somehow managed to get a ringside seat, and it was everything to me knowing he was right there next to me in my biggest moment, just like he had been my whole career.

Over the four two-minute rounds, I handily outpointed Russo, 17–9, using my speed, quicker punches, and superior ring generalship to dominate him.

"We got one down," Virg said to me over the phone that night after I got back to my room in the Olympic Village. "Now we're off to the next one."

The next challenge would be against the Russian: Makarenko. It was the biggest fight of my life. As I mentioned, he was a two-time world champion and the odds-on favorite to win the light heavyweight gold medal. I had already had a brief encounter with him before we got in the ring. I was riding to the arena and Makarenko got on the same bus. Makarenko had only heard whispers about me, but this was the first time we were face-to-face. He looked me up and down and smirked as though to say, *Dude, you're tiny.* I knew what that look was, and I resented it.

I stepped into the ring against him as the underdog—and I boxed my tail off that night, possibly my best amateur fight ever. Makarenko was six inches taller than me and rangy, with a special right hand. I could see right away why he was a two-time world champ. He was the truth. I opened up a 7–3 lead after the first round by using my first line of defense, my legs and footwork. My quickness was a problem for him—this allowed me to avoid his long-vaunted right hand and counter when he missed. In the second round I picked him up and lifted him off the mat coming out of a clinch; I needed to show him that though he was six inches taller than me, I was not going to be bullied, and that he wasn't the stronger fighter. Elite athletes don't always need to be taught new things in big moments—they need to be reminded of the things they already know. Coach Abdullah did just that for me. He never panicked. He gave me the instructions I needed when I needed them. At the final bell, I had amassed a 23–16 lead and scored the biggest upset in the Games at that point. It was Makarenko's first loss in five years.

The win sent shockwaves through the Olympic Village and the amateur boxing community. Who was this kid from the United States who dominated the menacing Makarenko? After that quarterfinal victory, I started getting a lot more attention at the Games. But I couldn't get too high because I still had two fights left before the gold medal.

In the meantime, I was watching my teammates drop off one by one. With every loss, the pressure on me to win a gold medal mounted. Nobody wants to go down in history as a medal-less team. We would never hear the end of it. I didn't want that for our coaches either. No one really expected much from us, but we didn't want to prove them right.

My win against Makarenko secured me a medal, but not the color I wanted. I found myself in the semifinals against Haydarov, a thirty-year-old southpaw. He was a tough, crafty veteran who had won the world title as a middleweight earlier in his career and fought in the 2000 Olympics. It turned out to be a close fight; I beat him 17–15. I had finally earned the coveted spot in the light heavyweight gold medal bout.

Leading up to the fight, I was getting a steady stream of phone calls. The United States had not had a boxer win a gold medal since light middleweight David Reid in 1996 (Abdullah's fighter). There was a great deal of anticipation that I might end the U.S. drought. I was ready, confident, anxious to get it done.

The day of the gold medal bout finally arrived, and everything seemed to be going wrong. That night, I only slept a few hours before it was time to leave for the venue. I felt off the whole day. I had assumed I was supposed to feel my best when moments like this arrived, but that wasn't the case for me. It wasn't nerves, it just seemed nothing was falling into place around me. Some of this adversity followed me into the ring.

Halfway through the gold medal bout, my opponent, Magomed Aripgadzhiyev, thumbed me in my right eye by accident. Right away, my vision got blurry and I could feel the eye starting to close. I moved around, staying away from him, as I tried to disguise what had happened. It couldn't have come at a worse time. I was down 9–7 at the end of the second round, but I had to shake it off. I was in the fight of my life. I had two more rounds to turn things around.

Coach Abdullah coached another great fight. We got the score-cards between rounds, so we knew I was behind. His composure was contagious.

"We need this now," he told me when I was behind. "We have to step this up."

Coach Abdullah's urgency gave me the jolt that I needed to shake off the nerves and fight my fight. I clawed my way back into to the fight, leading after the third round. As I sat in the corner, I realized that only one round stood between me and my gold medal.

I leapt off my stool—it was time to finish strong and leave no doubt. These moments are what every champion dreams about, having to dig deep, pull something special from inside, and find a way to win—and I was able to do just that.

When the final bell rang, the score was 20–13. I did it. I was an Olympic champion.

"I did it, Pop," I said when they interviewed me after the fight. "I know you're looking down on me. I love you." I'd beaten the odds to make it to this moment in my life. I had overcome all the trials and tribulations I had been through. I fulfilled the dream that Virg and my father had for me. I wasn't a failure; I'd finished what my father started.

I'd reached the pinnacle of amateur boxing success and was eager to make my debut as a professional. I celebrated my Olympic win with a victory lap around the country, taking meetings, shaking a lot of hands, and kissing babies.

The top managers in the sport had been coming after me for some time now, pitching their services and telling me everything I wanted to hear. "You're a great fighter—a sure shot to become a world champion." I was offered money on many occasions during my amateur career. It was just part of the game, but early on, I did not feel comfortable taking money from anyone. There is no structure in amateur boxing. It's not like the former NCAA rules, where there are guidelines prohibiting agents and managers from approaching you. In amateur boxing, if the sharks can get to you, they will. Often the socioeconomic background and lack of business and legal knowledge of fighters creates a feeding ground for managers and promoters to take advantage of them. But things felt different with James Prince. Prince managed Floyd Mayweather and advised Roy Jones Jr. in their respective careers. Prince was the front-runner to sign me, but there were other big managers who weren't far behind, like Shelly Finkel and Cameron Dunkin.

Prince has a reputation that extends far beyond boxing. He is a man who is respected, and some would even say feared. Other managers had to do their job to pursue the only American gold medalist. They did not want to disrespect him, but not even Prince could make these old dogs learn new tricks. There was a distinct difference between the way Prince pursued me and the way other managers made their pitches. They never talked to me about my personal life—it was strictly boxing. With Prince, we had a lot more in common: faith, family, and *then* boxing. I only heard from the other managers when it was time to talk business or when I was fighting in tournaments. Always promising the world, but the connection just didn't seem to be there. I wasn't just looking for a mouthpiece to represent me; I needed someone I could trust and bond with to help me navigate these shark-infested waters.

He understood where I came from. He was also a man of faith. Prince and I built a rapport after that first phone call a few years before.

I felt comfortable to the point where I had already told him that I would sign with him when I turned pro. In hindsight, that wasn't a wise thing to do; I effectively negotiated against myself.

He had seen and heard a lot over the years and had run into plenty of fighters who would make promises but not follow through. But I was a man of my word to a fault.

Prince commanded respect wherever he went. He had a real aura that the other managers couldn't bring. When you move around with Prince, you're moving with ten to twenty guys on any given day. When he walked into a room, you could see and feel the respect that he garnered. As a young man, I felt invincible when I was with him—especially when I was in Houston. Prince had foreign cars and big houses, and most of the guys around him had jewelry, cars, and reputations that preceded them. I respected that. At that time in my life, that's what got my attention. Shelly Finkel and Cameron Dunkin didn't have a shot.

Virg recommended that I sign with Prince because Prince had shown that he was willing to look after me. He and Virg met two years before the Olympics. Virg knew I was aware of Prince because he was Floyd Mayweather's manager, and I looked up to Floyd as a fighter. Prince reached out to Virg first, and Virg was able to get a feel for him. Virg had a lot of managers and advisers calling him, but he never really felt comfortable with any of them. Prince was the first manager Virg felt comfortable enough to sit down and engage in conversation without feeling that there was some sort of trick up his sleeve. Ultimately, Virg felt Prince could be trusted. Virg knew several fighters who were cheated by promoters, and Prince went and got their money for them. He actually took the promoters to court, which showed Virg that he would fight for me.

Going with Prince wasn't a popular decision with a lot of people, even some of my family members. When Uncle Bob got wind of it, he tried to talk me out of it.

"This guy's got a reputation, Dre," he said. Bob wanted me to choose Finkel.

I did my homework on Prince but I didn't dig too deep into his reputation. I didn't feel the need to. I judged him by who I saw him to be at the time, not by his past. I judged him by the way he treated me and my family. I had heard negative stories about most of the promoters and managers in boxing. The realization was that no matter which manager or promoter I ended up working with, none were squeaky clean; I just needed to choose the best fit for me.

As I was preparing to return home after the Olympics, Virg advised me to go to Houston first. I didn't really know why, but I trusted his guidance.

Later that night I was on the phone with Tiff and told her what Virg said.

"Go to Houston for what?" she asked.

"I don't know. He wants to make sure everything is right before I come home."

I had never won a gold medal, so this was all new to me. I didn't have any reason to question it. I was seeking counsel and advice from the people who mattered to me.

"Look, go to Houston, but don't sign anything," Tiff said.

"Alright. I got you. I won't sign anything."

When I was in Houston, I spent a lot of time with Prince at his ranch. While he and I were talking, he made his move. Prince threw a big stack of cash on the bed. This was the seed money for an eventual six-figure signing bonus.

"That's just the beginning," he said. "There's gonna be a lot more where this came from."

He had a contract in his hand. If I signed right there, the money on the bed and the rest of the signing bonus would be mine.

I turned the money down on that first day. It didn't feel right. "Nah, J, I gotta think on this, man. Let me go back to my hotel room and sleep on it."

He shrugged. "Alright, cool," he said. "Let's talk tomorrow."

I called Tiff and told her what had happened.

"Dre, don't sign anything," she repeated. She knew it would be premature for me to sign a contract without at least having a lawyer look at it. But I didn't see it. I went back to Prince's house the next day and signed the contract.

The truth is that my loyalty and my need to keep my word were driving me to sign, more than the money. Years later as I reflect on that moment, I learned two valuable lessons. First, it's not about loyalty, it's about business. I should never have signed a binding contract without representation. I owed it to myself to review the financial figures and other terms. The second and biggest lesson I learned from that moment was that you don't get what's right, you don't get what's fair, *you get what you negotiate.* I made up my mind that something like this would never happen again—and for the rest of my career, it never did.

I don't regret signing with Prince—but I regret signing that initial contract he offered. My failure to negotiate would become the source of much strife (and a lawsuit) between me and Prince. The more knowledgeable I became about contracts and more importantly, my contracts, the more holes I began to spot. But in 2004, I did not have the business acumen needed to compete with Prince on that level. I knew enough to read my contract, but I didn't know the deeper things to look for. There were specific deal points that I knew to check for, like my signing bonus and fight minimums, but I didn't know to look for things such as jurisdiction or hidden extensions that are customary in all boxing contracts. These can be triggered by an injury or winning a world title.

When I got home, Tiffiney said, "You said you weren't going to sign anything, Dre."

"I know, I know. I'm sorry. I felt like it was a good deal." I showed her the bag full of money.

She wasn't moved by the money. She was mad at me for signing so quickly. To this day, she's still mad at me for signing that first deal with Prince. As for Virg, I think he was enamored by it all too. He'd never signed a professional contract, either, or provided counsel on one. It all sounded like a lot of money. In addition, I had just gotten $25,000 from the U.S. Olympic Committee for winning the gold medal. Virg came to me and reminded me of all the money he had invested in my amateur career, so I gave him $10,000. I had no idea if that was a fair amount; but I did know Virg was responsible for a lot of my success, and he had spent a lot of money on me for me to get to this point, so I gave him the money.

Now that my manager was secured, we both were on the hunt for the right promoter. I went on a mini tour, talking to all the big-name boxing promoters. Ricardo Williams, the 2000 Olympic silver medalist, had previously signed a seven-figure payday right out of the Olympics. But as I mentioned, trouble with the law landed him in federal prison. His legal issues and the belief that the 2000 class had gotten too much too soon now had the promoters, the networks, and the managers spooked. What happened in 2000 caused a significant pay cut in my signing bonus. The industry had changed drastically in the last four years. A gold medal no longer came with a seven-figure signing bonus, and I would have to do more to earn my way to that point. Prince and I went to New York and had a meeting with Don King. I knew Prince and Don had a history between them, and there seemed to be mutual respect between the two. Don walked into the hotel lobby draped in jewelry and wearing his customary "Only in America" denim jacket, covered with a bunch of images of his face and the American flag.

"What's up, brotha?" he said. "How you doin'?"

Before the meeting, Prince had warned me: "We ain't signing with none of these dudes yet." When he said it, in the back of my mind I was thinking, *Yeah, but you weren't saying that when I signed with you.* The meeting with Don lasted for about two hours—and Don basically talked the whole time. Brotha this, brotha that.

"Brotha, you know the American dream is winning that gold medal," he said. "Brotha, we gonna make you a household name and a superstar. And you're sitting down with the right one—tell him, Prince!"

He just kept talking and talking. At a certain point, Prince interrupted, "I hear you, King. I hear you. Let's get to business and talk about this contract. So tell me this, how much do you have in mind as a bonus for Dre?"

"Brotha, whatever you want to put on that contract, we can put on that contract," King said. "You tell me the number, brotha. We gon' put it on there and we gon' sign it."

Me and Prince looked at each other. We both almost fell out laughing, but we held it together; this was still a business meeting. My next thought was, *This dude is crazy. He's running game.* But we saw straight through it.

When we finally did get an offer from Don, it was so low, so insulting, that we never countered—we never even responded.

ELEVEN

PRIZEFIGHTING

We settled on a West Coast promoter named Dan Goossen who had promoted fighters like Mike Tyson, James Toney, and Bernard Hopkins. We felt a West Coast promoter was good for me because I wanted to be heavily promoted in the Bay Area and the West Coast in general. We also brought in the legendary Roy Jones Jr. as my co-promoter. Roy was my favorite fighter and he had his own promotional company, Square Ring. We strategically put Roy and the CEO of his company, Brad Jacobs, in place as another set of eyes and ears to ensure the numbers and terms that were being presented to us were real.

My first professional fight was a week before Christmas—December 18, 2004. It was televised on HBO, which was a big deal. Without a gold medal, a young fighter typically has to fight for years before having a fight shown on HBO. That night I fought on the undercard of the Antonio Tarver–Glen Johnson light heavyweight championship fight. Chris Molina was my opponent, a boxer out of Texas who was very unknown. Virg wanted us to pick fighters who would provide enough of a test so I could develop as a young pro, but he didn't want me to be rushed along the way.

The night of the fight I was nervous but also excited. This was the first step in a pro career, and there was a lot of pressure from the boxing world. There was no headgear; I wore no tank top. This was different. I felt bare, naked. The first time I had pulled on a professional pair of gloves, I was shocked by how minimal the padding was. I could literally see and feel my knuckles through the glove. *Man, we're fighting in these?* They were so thin that if you blocked a hard punch with the gloves, you could still feel the impact of the punch through the gloves. It wasn't like that with the big, bulky amateur gloves. The reality of it all hit me—this was a different game.

As I made my first walk to the ring, I noticed right away that the crowd was different than what I was used to. They wanted blood. But my nerves started to dissipate after I landed the first few punches. The crowd oohed and aahed as I began to overwhelm Molina with speed and power. I started to realize that even though the crowd was bigger and that there was more pressure on me, at the end of the day, this was still just boxing. I turned up the heat on Molina until I scored a technical knockout (TKO) in the second round. I was so relieved that I got my first fight out of the way without any mishaps.

My purse for that first fight was made public: $250,000. The very next day, I had a family member ask me for money. I let them know I couldn't do it. It was a quick introduction to my new life. In many ways, this situation is unique to professional athletes because the details of our contracts are open to the eyes of the public. People quickly saw dollar signs. And I got my first taste of the pressure and difficulties I would be experiencing for the next decade.

Tiff and I knew we wanted to save and invest, but we didn't really know what that meant. We had the desire, but we didn't have the knowledge. Early on I leaned heavily on Prince. I'm a visual learner, so I watched how Prince moved money around and of course I asked a lot of questions. I started out by using one of his financial advisers. I knew I didn't want to be broke at the end of my career. Figuring out how to avoid that would take time. Tiff was a big help—she's the smartest person I know. She has an innate instinct with money and a good grip on saving and not overspending. But it was a learning journey for both of us.

Two months after that first fight, I was out there again, this time against Kenny Kost, who fought out of St. Paul, Minnesota. This was a big step up from my first opponent. He was a good fighter with a strong amateur background. He was experienced, with an 8–0 record. At the end of the first round, Kost hit me with an uppercut, which was my kryptonite at the time. I didn't know how to defend against an uppercut in the pro ranks. I was still shedding ten years of bad habits from being in the amateurs: dropping my hands at certain times, leaping in with my punches while leaving my chin exposed to get hit. I would relax too much on the inside of a clinch, believing my opponent wouldn't take advantage. But he did. These veterans knew how to shoot that uppercut when I wasn't expecting it. When I got buzzed, I wobbled back and grabbed him. I knew what to do when I got hurt in a fight. My father used to teach me when I was a young kid. I recovered, gained my composure, and ended up winning a unanimous decision in the six-round fight.

I fought about six or seven times that year. That was the normal pace of a young fighter gaining experience, winning, and taking little punishment in fights along the way. I was ready to fight anybody. I was also trying to find my way in the pro game while trying to please the media and network's appetite to see me fight someone real—so they could see if I had what it took at the next level. Virg had an old-school mentality: protect your fighter from being rushed until both the trainer and fighter feel they are ready to step up. Once you make the leap from fighting guys no one knows to fighting contenders, there is no going back. Timing is everything. Not to mention many careers have been ruined by a fighter taking the wrong fight one or two fights too soon. But the suits at HBO knew they would make more money by putting me in big fights against big names.

When they presented my next opponent, Darnell Boone, and I watched the film that they sent over, there wasn't anything spectacular about what I saw, but for some reason I got a bad feeling about him. I can't explain what it was. It wasn't fear—there was nothing scary about the dude—but something didn't feel right. I wasn't built, trained, or raised to turn down an opponent. It is contrary to my mental makeup. I didn't say a word to Virg, and he didn't seem bothered by Boone at all. He was only pointing out Boone's mistakes: "He's punching over his feet; he's got bad technique. You're going to tear him up," Virg said.

I believed him. I still did not feel at total peace about it, but we accepted the fight anyway. As a fighter, you learn to suppress negative thoughts, emotions, and feelings. Physically, I had a good training camp, but deep down I continued to feel like more adversity was ahead.

We arrived in Portland, Oregon, a week before the fight to get acclimated.

My fight was another six rounder and was on the undercard of the Floyd Mayweather–Sharmba Mitchell fight on HBO. My co-promoter, Roy Jones Jr., was calling the fight at ringside for the network. As I sat in the locker room, I was thinking that it was just nerves I was feeling: the normal anxiety before a fight, nothing more. I convinced myself I was ready, even though I was unsettled. I knew it wasn't that I was afraid of this dude. That wasn't it. I felt I was going to beat him.

Through the first three rounds, I was boxing well, getting in my shots, avoiding most of his big, desperate punches. In the fourth round, my amateur mistakes finally caught up with me. In the amateurs, when you get into a clinch, you are taught to stop when the referee says "break." You have to respect the referee's command—if you don't, you could lose a point. Virg had been in my ear about it since I entered the pro ranks, but I had many years of bad habits I was trying to shake. "Man, you have to stop getting lackadaisical on the inside. One of these guys is going to crack you one day," he had predicted.

With thirty-six seconds left in the fourth round, Boone put everything he had into an uppercut to the chin that I didn't see coming. *Boom!* I went down hard on my stomach. I stumbled to my feet and moved around, trying to clear my head, doing whatever I could to survive that round.

The bell rang to close out round four. I had made it. I've never admitted this to anybody—except Tiffiney—but the last two rounds of this fight are completely erased from my memory. I don't remember anything from the moment that I went down in the fourth round until the moment the referee raised my hand in victory. I heard a chorus of both cheers and boos. Otherwise, it is all a blank to me. I don't remember what Virg told me in the corner. It was only God and my boxing instincts that got me through the rest of the fight.

In boxing, the kill shot is the one that you don't see. I didn't see that shot; I wasn't braced for it. If I had known it was coming, I could have broken the punch in half, or tucked my chin so the punch would not have landed cleanly—something to lessen the impact. Truth be told, those are the kind of punches that, if landed right, would knock many fighters out cold.

I was a Jordan athlete—I had been chosen to represent the Jordan Brand for Nike. There was a great deal of pressure on me that night—not just to win, but also to look good while winning. All Boone had to do was look half decent and he would get pats on the back and a call for another big fight. I had to continue to look like a rising star. The late, great Naazim Richardson, the legendary trainer from Philadelphia, used to always say, "Dre, early in your career is going to be the hardest times for you; you are fighting guys who have nothing to lose, but you have everything to lose." Naazim was right.

When you get knocked down in boxing, a lot of fans will automatically think you lost, despite what the scorecards say. The truth is, many people don't really know what they're looking at when they watch a fight. Since my early teens, I've never had the luxury of having an off night while fighting. This comes with winning a lot; even a close fight can feel like a loss for me. Now that I was a professional, the standard was multiplied exponentially. This standard brings a great deal of pressure and anxiety. I learned over the years to shoulder the pressure and keep a smile on my face. After the Boone fight, I started to see the looks of disappointment on my team's faces. Their expressions told me *You didn't perform well tonight.*

A few days after the fight, I got my first introduction to the ruthlessness of professional prizefighting. For the first time in my career, I started seeing negative headlines like, "Maybe Ward Is Not Who We Thought He Was." I understood this position to a point. What I did not understand was why I didn't read many articles about how I got off the canvas and finished the fight strong. The media only saw it one way. I do acknowledge that the optics didn't look good. Though I was hurt in that moment, I had to grow up and realize that not everybody was going to like me. The same dudes who were begging for interviews would switch up in the blink of an eye and start to attack me. I tried to process what was happening. I was mad at myself.

Tiff was trying to encourage me, to help me. "Baby, look, you got through it. God got you through it with your hand raised."

But I still sat in that anger for a while. All the press I had gotten up to that point—after the Olympics and during the first year of my professional career—had been positive. The only negativity I ever heard was, "Ward has an amateur style and doesn't have a lot of power." The media never wrote anything about my character because they didn't really know me. But when I got knocked down, everything shifted, not just with the media, but also in my heart. I learned that many in the media are opportunists. From that point forward, I began to develop a wall of distrust that would only grow over the next decade. For months, I continued to deal with writers and pundits stating one of the worst things you could say about a fighter: he doesn't have a chin, meaning that I couldn't take a punch. They wondered whether I had received too much praise coming out of the Olympics and would I be a bust. Boone was also out there running his mouth to anyone who would listen that he had beaten me, which compounded the negativity I was getting. It was the worst feeling I had experienced in my short pro career up to that point. I won the fight—and it had been years since I had lost a fight—but what I was dealing with in that moment felt like a loss. I couldn't stand it. I was so competitive and wanted to shine every time I stepped in that ring.

My next big fight was Andy Kolle, another test for me—a real sink-or-swim moment. I knew deep down that if I fumbled the ball, so to speak, I would be officially labeled a bust. I'd come too far and couldn't let that happen. Kolle, who was from Minnesota, was 9–0. As the fight got closer, we continued to hear noise in the boxing world about my chin. Virg felt the need to address it with me.

"Son, I know you can take a punch," he said. "I've seen you spar too many times. Taking a punch is not just physical, it's a mindset."

He was teaching me the kind of mental focus and resolve I needed to make it in the pro game—at a time when they were starting to question whether I had the goods. The fight against Kolle was my moment. If I didn't win, I don't think Andre Ward would have ever become *Andre Ward*.

When I stepped into the ring that night at the Foxwoods Resort Casino in Connecticut, I was fully confident, locked in, and at peace. I knew I was about to dog him. Virg had me wired—*I don't care what you hit me with, I'm not going anywhere.* I smiled and winked at the camera on my way to the ring. That was bad news for Mr. Kolle. I made him quit at the end of the sixth round of the eight-round fight. I took a few good shots, and I took them well. But I dished out a lot more than I received; I shined that night. The HBO commentators generally praised my performance, though Max Kellerman still called my chin "suspect" during the fight.

I continued my march through the ranks with a string of TKOs— seven in a row. By now I had moved up from middleweight to super middleweight; this was eight pounds north of the 160-pound weight class I had been fighting in. This was a better fit for my body, which was still growing and filling out.

Virg was steadily working on my inside fighting skills, knowing I would need that as I stepped up in competition. Virg told me, "The only style that can give you problems in the ring is a buzz-saw-type style—a guy who stays up close to you and smothers you. You will be a good fighter if you only fight on the outside. But you will become great if you learn how to fight more than one way."

Stamina and physical strength are two tools you need for effective inside fighting. I already had those two covered. I had to learn how to slip in and get past the opponent's punches, to smother his range. Once inside, I had to learn what punches to use, be able to use my feet to reset my position—all while staying up close to the other guy.

Acquiring the skills required repetition until it became second nature, but I didn't always like the work that was required. It was awkward at first. It was tedious, detailed, and unfamiliar. Virg forced me to keep working day in and day out. He had the foresight to know that this was the piece of the puzzle that would be needed for me to win and keep a championship for a long time.

One of my greatest weapons over the span of my career was that I was constantly underestimated. I benefitted from people's misperceptions of who I was. A lot of this was fueled by what the media said and wrote about me. Because I was a gold medalist, people wrongly assumed that everything was given to me. Many opponents would acknowledge my skill set but thought I wasn't tough or physically strong. That was the furthest thing from the truth.

In 2008, HBO approached Prince with the opportunity for me to fight Allan Green or Edison Miranda—both dangerous contenders—for substantially more money than I had ever seen in my pro career.

"We can beat them, don't get me wrong," Virg told me. "But I need you to build up a little bit more man strength. When we do fight these kinds of guys, I don't just want you to outbox them, I want you to destroy them. We want to dominate. This time next year we'll take these fights."

That's exactly what we did. But it was taboo in the sport of boxing to turn down opportunities like that, especially when it's your first big call. Virg was not just my boxing coach or a hired hand; he was my godfather. The bond was much deeper. His responsibility to help guide my career and to not allow the suits to rush me ran deep. Virg was raised by trainers who taught him that his ultimate purpose as a head trainer was to help his fighter get home safely to his family. We both were also students of the game—not just the fighting part, but also the business side. I couldn't tell you how many young fighters we saw get pressured into jumping in the deep end against tougher competition and it backfired. We've seen many young careers ruined in the sport by taking the wrong fight too early.

When we turned HBO down, Prince, always the businessman, asked, "Are you sure? We don't know when they're going to come back to us with another opportunity."

"We just need to keep doing what we're doing," Virg responded. "Dre is going to be running the game real soon. When we do fight these guys, if they're still there, we will get twice as much money."

Virg turned out to be exactly right about that. But at the time, I was torn. I trusted Virg like a father; he had never lied to me. But I knew I would have to deal with the media backlash as soon as word got out to the press. Fighters love to run to the press and holler, "He doesn't want to fight me!" But I couldn't worry about that—we were playing the long game.

TWELVE

SUPER SIX

When Prince told me that Showtime was organizing a tournament called the Super Six in 2009, none of us fully understood what it was. There had never been a six-man boxing tournament in the history of the sport. The closest thing boxing had ever seen was a Don King–promoted four-man, single-elimination tournament in the middleweight division in 2001. Prince tried to explain but it didn't sound right. Six different fighters, in a double-elimination, round-robin-style tournament? "Naw, that's not going to work," I said. "I'm not an amateur anymore—professionals don't fight in tournaments."

He rattled off the fighters who were going to be involved: myself; reigning super middleweight champions Mikkel Kessler from Denmark and Carl Froch from England; former middleweight champions Jermain Taylor from the United States and Arthur Abraham from Germany/Armenia; and 2004 U.S. Olympic bronze medalist Andre Dirrell, who is a close friend of mine and a fighter I had come up with through the amateur ranks. These were real fighters. These were the kind of fights I needed to break through and prove that I belonged, but these were also the kind of fighters that if I wasn't ready it was going to show. It was also hard to imagine that all these promoters, managers, fighters, and egos would be able to come together and pull this off. I trusted Prince's instincts, so when he told me he didn't think the tournament was going to come together, I believed him and moved on.

"Keep me in the loop if anything happens," I told him.

I took my family down to Mexico for a much-needed vacation in San Felipe, not far from San Diego. While I was there, I got a double ear infection; it was rough. I felt terrible. When I went online, I read that they were on the verge of announcing the Super Six in New York, with the first leg of the promotional tour in just a few days.

"Prince, what's up?" I asked when I got him on the phone. "I see that the tournament is going to be announced in New York."

"Yeah, I'm hearing that too. But I still don't believe it is going to happen," he said.

"Are you sure?" I asked.

"Yeah. Enjoy your vacation."

Another day went by, and I didn't hear from anybody. The next day, I read that the press conference would take place the following day. I had one day left of my vacation, but I knew I needed to get in contact with Virg.

"Listen to me," Virg told me. "This tournament is going to happen. We have to get you home and get you on a plane to the next stop on the press tour. I talked to Goossen. If you don't get on this plane and you miss this opportunity, it's not going to be good. There's gonna be repercussions if you don't go through with this."

"But I'm in Mexico with my family."

"Listen, baby, get on the plane—*now*," he said. I was upset that I had to end my vacation abruptly, but I did exactly what he told me to do. Anytime Virg spoke to me in that tone, he was typically right. I knew I needed to listen to him.

I looked online and saw that I missed the first announcement. My absence was not lost on anyone. People were asking, "Where is Ward? Is he a no-show? Is he not in this tournament?"

So now my absence was a thing. It was time to go. I packed up the car and we headed back to San Diego. As I drove back to the airport, I was still upset because I had gotten bad information and because I was sick. Now I had to abruptly leave my family and head to Germany for the next leg of the press tour as soon as we got back. I quickly unpacked one bag and frantically packed another to get back to the airport on time and board my red-eye flight to Germany.

When I arrived at the press conference in Germany, Froch, Abraham, and Kessler were extremely smug. I quickly realized that the three European fighters in the tournament were the favorites, and the three Americans were just there to make things interesting. I noticed right away that the European media was blatantly dismissive of the Americans. The prevailing perception was that Taylor was on the back end of his career and Dirrell and I were too green, and probably not ready for this level of competition. I took that personally. I had been taught from a young boy to use it as fuel and another source of motivation.

I called Virg that night from Germany.

"Virg, the media doesn't think that I have a shot to win this."

"That's what we want. That's the position we've always been in. Remember the Olympics—you got the toughest draw. They're not going to know what hit 'em."

One major stipulation was that everyone had to travel to an opponent's home country at least once. But when the negotiations were done, I was the only fighter who didn't have to travel overseas. I never once instructed my team to fight for this clause, nor did I direct them to fight for me to stay in the States. My attorney, Josh Dubin, and Prince did a phenomenal job for me at the negotiating table. I will never apologize for that. Over the years, I've heard some fans and media complain and grumble about me not having to fight on the road like the rest of the guys: "You didn't travel." "You're a homebody." "You were scared." Blah, blah, blah. What no one brings up is that I had the toughest first fight out of everyone in the tournament. Kessler was the top dog. The main reason Kessler didn't make me travel was arrogance. He was overconfident. I was a young pup with only twenty fights. He was a seasoned veteran, 42–1, who had more knockouts—thirty-two of them—than I had fights. Kessler and his team were so confident he would win that they agreed to fight me in my hometown of Oakland, California—and it backfired.

Kessler didn't think traveling to my backyard would matter. But I knew what he had gotten himself into—he was coming to the lion's den, and he wasn't ready. The media's take was that I was a good boxer, the Olympic gold medalist, and it was an "interesting" matchup, but that ultimately Kessler was too good and too experienced for me to beat him. Nobody complained about him fighting in Oakland—until the fight was over. Then I heard, "Oh, you didn't travel—it's not fair." As I've stated before, you don't get what's fair, you get what you negotiate. Boxing is a game of chess. You always have to be thinking two or three steps ahead.

Kessler came to the Bay Area about four weeks before the fight to get acclimated. I knew this because we tracked every significant move he made. Virg is old school; he always has his feelers out to get as much information on the enemy as possible. We knew when Kessler left Denmark; we knew when he landed in the Bay Area. We also became aware that he would be training at a gym in Sacramento, and we just so happened to know the good folks up north. We got reports about his training every day. What Kessler didn't know was that his camp had reached out to one of my chief sparring partners, Brandon Gonzáles, to be his sparring partner. Brandon would spar with me one day, then he would go back to Sacramento and spar with Kessler the next day. Typically, top fighters spar every other day, but Brandon was double-dipping. He was trying to get that money, and more opportunity, and I don't blame him one bit. Brandon stuck to the code, though, and came to us before he agreed to do it.

"Kessler's team reached out to me to spar, but I won't spar with him if you don't want me to," Brandon told Virg.

"No, I want you to spar with him," Virg responded. "But I'm gonna be talking to you and I need you to tell me everything that's going on."

"I got you, Virg," he said.

Brandon would give Virg regular updates: "I put hands on him today," he said one time. "I whipped this dude from pillar to post today," he said another time. "He's too slow. He can't beat Dre."

Kessler had no idea this was going on. But this was war—and in war, we need to know everything that we can about you. Everything. Because it all matters when you're talking about a game like boxing, a game of inches. No detail is too small. We continued to learn everything about Kessler, and he knew nothing about us. Our team was built on old-school principles. We never shared much about what we were doing. If we showed anything on camera, it was something basic, things we did not mind the public knowing. I never had a bunch of people around me in training camp because people talk—even good, well-meaning people talk. You practically had to be family before we'd tell you anything about our training camp. Media didn't like it, but that's how we moved, and it worked for us.

I knew that this was my moment—my opportunity to silence the critics who said I didn't have a chin, the ones who said I couldn't punch, the ones who felt like I had an amateur style and wasn't ready. The Super Six was a risky tournament for me to jump into at this early stage in my pro career, with just twenty fights. Kessler's only loss had been to future Hall of Famer Joe Calzaghe, a Welshman considered one of the best super middleweight fighters of all time. I was either going to come out of this tournament shining, or I would lose in the Super Six and perhaps ruin my career and confirm all the negative things that had been said about me.

Two weeks before the fight, I started feeling the nerves, but I think it was mostly excitement. This is typically when my sleep during training camp would be disrupted. My mind was fixated on the fight even when I was asleep. There would be times when I would wake up in cold sweats. This was confirmation that the fight was close. This would be my first world title fight, and a win would validate everything I had done in my career since I was ten years old. I don't know what I was more excited about, fighting for a world title or this fight being in my hometown. The city of Oakland was buzzing with crazy energy from all the prefight excitement. Everywhere I went, I felt it. We didn't have to go to Vegas; we brought Vegas to the Bay.

Social media wasn't as big yet in 2009, so that wasn't a focal point, but there was still a lot of activity on Twitter. When Kessler and I encountered each other at prefight events, I continued to see his smug arrogance.

"You see the look on his face?" Virg whispered in my ear.

"Yeah, I see it."

"He just can't fathom you beating him," he said. "That's why he came to Oakland, Dre."

Virg had a gift for reading my opponents like a book; then he would give me the play and I would execute. People think boxing is just about training, working out, and getting your body prepared, but your psyche is also a major part of your preparation. Virg watched Kessler's team all week and constantly stayed in my ear, telling me all the right things to keep me fired up.

"Look at them. They expect you to be happy just to be here. But Kessler doesn't know we are about to tear him up. He just doesn't know."

I had the prefight press conference at City Hall in downtown Oakland. They built a stage right in front of the City Hall entrance, and the plaza was overflowing with hundreds of people. Every time I did a face-off with Kessler, I made a point to look through him. I wanted Kessler to feel me, to know I was serious. As I've said, I've never been the rah-rah guy who does a lot of talking. I make my point and mean it. I was raised to have substance and back up my words. I wasn't going to talk just to sell a fight and then not be able to back it up. I think I got a lot of that from my father. Ironically, most of my heroes in the game did a whole bunch of talking—Ali, Floyd Mayweather, Bernard Hopkins, Roy Jones Jr. They talked, but they almost always backed it up. I can do that if I need to—I can talk with the best of them—but my nature is that I don't like to waste words. When I speak, I want people to listen.

The day before the fight was the weigh-in. When I got to the stage, I looked out and saw more cameras than I had ever seen in my life—even more than the Olympics. It was crazy. This is when the magnitude of this moment really hit me.

"This is it," Virg said in my ear. "You feel them goosebumps?"

That got me even more locked in. I looked out and saw people I hadn't seen in years. All my boxing brothers were there: Kevin Cunningham from St. Louis, Barry Hunter and the Peterson brothers from DC, Uncle Andre Rozier from New York. I saluted them. There were so many people from my past. I loved it. Seeing my people energized me. It was almost time to show out and do my thing.

Later that night, I needed to get out of the hotel, so I went to the store to walk off some nerves and clear my head. I called Uncle Bob, the person who had the closest connection to my dad.

"Sonny Boy," he said, using the name he always called me by, "this is it." Tears rolled down my cheeks as I listened to him. I felt every word he was saying. "Man, your dad would be so proud," he said.

"I know," I answered.

"I have no doubt that you're gonna do it," he continued. "And I'm getting to the arena early. I'm gonna be right there, front and center."

I slept great—the best sleep I'd ever had before a big fight. I felt like I literally didn't move until the morning. When I woke up, the first thought that popped in my head was, *It's fight day!* I jumped out of bed and felt a great, calming peace. I wasn't fearful or overly anxious. I felt the love all around me, like this was all meant to be—like everything was already written. That's what Virg would always tell me. I just needed to walk into it.

When I got to the Oracle Arena (now called the Oakland Arena), I could feel the energy of the place reverberating off the walls like sound waves. I wore red, white, and blue trunks, representing the United States. But I also represented Christ—the words "Jesus Christ Is King" were printed on the back of my robe in big, red letters. With everything that I been through, everything I had to overcome to get to this point—my upbringing, the drugs and alcohol, the streets—I felt like I was *here*, in *this* moment, for such a time as this. And I was going to give God the glory.

Brandon, my sparring partner, had sent me a text the night before that confirmed what I was already feeling: HE CAN'T BEAT YOU.

It was in all caps, just those four words. When the fight began, I was ready for whatever Kessler was going to bring. And I showed out.

Kessler had some good moments, but I had too much flavor for him. He was a good fighter, but he was straight up and down in that European style. While he was very technically sound, he only came at me one way—and he wasn't going to beat me that way. I used my speed, my flavor, and my IQ. I took away his greatest strengths and exposed his weaknesses. Virg coached just like I knew he would that night; I fought just like I knew I could that night. The fight was stopped midway through the eleventh round because of a serious cut to Kessler's eye that was caused by an accidental headbutt. When they went to the scorecards, I was far ahead according to all three judges—97-93, 98-92, 98-92—and was now the new World Boxing Association (WBA) super middleweight champion.

"I'm sure that somewhere, Frank Ward is watching and is very proud of his son," commentator Gus Johnson told the Showtime audience after they announced the decision.

The arena exploded. My two boys, Andre Jr. and Malachi, now eight and six, joined me in the ring; I gave them big kisses as they watched me celebrate. I hugged my mother. Her presence made this moment even sweeter.

After the fight, Kessler's team complained about two headbutts, but they were both accidental contact. I dominated the fight, stinging Kessler repeatedly with rights and lefts. A headbutt can't cause as much damage as you saw on his face. When you watch the video, Kessler didn't complain when the fight was stopped. He walked away; he was ready to get out of that ring and out of Oakland. All of the complaining came afterward. This would become a theme for every big fight I won in my career. First there would be doubt, then the excuses would follow after I dominated the fight. I learned to ignore it—it was just part of the game.

My victory over Kessler shocked a lot of people. I think a majority of the boxing world thought I was going to lose. After all, Kessler was the favorite to win the whole tournament, and rightfully so. It was a blessing that I fought him first. I was sending a message to the rest of the fighters in the field that I wasn't just there to take part in the Super Six; I was there to take *over*.

THIRTEEN

CROWNED

Next up was Allan Green, a boxer from Oklahoma who didn't get a lot of love from the media. He was a dark horse in the tournament, someone who wasn't expected to make a lot of noise. But I knew he was a tough fighter. Originally, I was supposed to fight Jermain Taylor, but he withdrew from the Super Six after getting knocked out by Arthur Abraham in Germany.

Green had—in brutal fashion—knocked out a guy I came up with, Jaidon Codrington, and pretty much ruined his career. I knew Green was a bad man. He was dangerous, probably a tougher opponent than Taylor at that point.

Green came in mean-mugging, trying to intimidate me, but that wasn't going to work. That fight saw the birth of Andre Ward, the inside fighter.

I hadn't seen the value in working on my inside game, but it showed up in this fight in a major way. I was previously known as just a skilled boxer but no one really knew me as a strong inside fighter, not even Green. I bullied him all over the ring. I pinned him against the ropes and he couldn't move. It was a revelation for me. I dogged him with my inside fighting. I beat him up. I won every round on all three scorecards. My only regret was that I didn't knock him out.

I was scheduled to face Andre Dirrell next. Dirrell's trainer and grandfather, Bumper, had been close to me and Virg for a long time. Throughout our careers, Virg and Bumper would always try to avoid us fighting each other. When they announced that Dirrell and I would both be in the Super Six, it gave Virg some angst. I wasn't as concerned. I wasn't eager to fight Dirrell, but I was game if it was necessary. I knew he was a bad man, with fast hands and feet. He was sometimes awkward in his movements; his nickname was "The Matrix." I was more fundamentally sound, but he might have had more natural ability. We'd sparred once at the Olympic Training Center. Neither of us really dominated the sparring session, but I was very familiar with his skill set. I knew Virg and Bumper were talking about how they could avoid the fight, but I tried to stay away from all of that—I knew I had to keep my mind right. *We are going to fight, and they are not going to be able to stop it.*

But as it happened, we didn't have to fight after all. Before we could fight, Dirrell had to first beat hard-hitting Arthur Abraham. I traveled to Detroit to watch the fight at Joe Louis Arena. Detroit was a major fight town with a lot of energy around boxing. They came out heavy for Dirrell. I watched from ringside as he boxed while Abraham kept barely missing him with big punches. Dirrell knocked Abraham down in the fourth round. When Dirrell slipped on the mat in the eleventh, Abraham punched him in the head while he was down, a clear foul. Dirrell stayed on the mat; he looked to be out cold, and bedlam ensued in the arena. It felt like the entire Detroit crowd was trying to get in the ring to go after Abraham, but his cheap shot ultimately got him disqualified. Dirrell, who'd been way ahead on the scorecards at the time of the stoppage, was announced the winner.

When Dirrell did a post-fight interview with commentator Jim Gray, he cried out, "I don't know what happened, man!" He didn't seem to have all of his faculties. Dirrell eventually withdrew from the tournament for unknown medical reasons. I felt bad for him. This was a big opportunity for both of us, and it all ended abruptly.

In place of fighting Dirrell next, I had to fight Sakio Bika from Cameroon as a replacement, though it wasn't considered a Super Six tournament fight. I wasn't really feeling this news. *Nobody* wanted to fight Sakio Bika. It was a lose-lose situation. This dude was physically strong and blatantly dirty. He would hit you with an elbow, headbutt you, or hit you on the back of the head and wouldn't think anything of it. I didn't know which was worse—fighting my boy Dirrell or fighting Bika.

As I predicted, the fight was ugly. I still did my thing, controlling the fight from start to finish, but at moments it turned into a wrestling match. I needed to do whatever it took to get and keep my respect from Bika. He is the type who will steamroll any form of weakness.

After I won, the Showtime commentators Gus Johnson, Antonio Tarver, and Al Bernstein praised my performance. They called the fight ugly but said I showed toughness and a chameleon-like style to win such a match.

Even though he had lost by disqualification to Dirrell, the Super Six tournament was double elimination, so I fought Arthur Abraham in the semifinal round. Just like before the Darnell Boone fight, things felt a little off for me before the fight. I've always battled with Virg about what time we will get to the venue on fight night. Virg wants to get there as early as possible. But once you get to the venue, you can't eat or drink anything except water. The commissioner has to shadow you to make sure you don't slip anything into your system. But on that night, I didn't take into consideration LA traffic when I decided what time I would leave the hotel to head to the venue. Carson, California, is about eighteen miles south of LA—but that eighteen miles might take anywhere from twenty minutes to over an hour, depending on traffic. I ended up getting to the arena late, which meant everything had to be rushed. I was scheduled to walk to the ring at 8:30, but I didn't get there until 6:45. I'd never been rushed before a pro fight and I didn't like how it felt. It made me uneasy.

The fight was taking place at an outdoor arena and it was chilly that night—about sixty degrees. Carson has a heavy Armenian population, and Abraham is Armenian so it seemed at times like he was fighting in front of his home crowd.

The worst thing to happen before the fight involved the referee, Luis Pabon of Puerto Rico. He came into my locker room to give his prefight instructions, and the way he talked to me and my team, we knew we were going to have a tough time with him. Typically when a referee goes over all the rules for the fight, they will allow each team to ask any questions or voice any concerns. But the first thing that Pabon came in and said was, "I want you to know something—I'm not putting up with none of that roughhousing in there tonight." I was confused.

Virg and I looked at each other. *What did he just say?* Clearly, I was acquiring a reputation because of the rough inside fighting I had been doing recently, particularly in the Bika fight. But I had *never* heard a ref say something like this to me. Normally they'd be more coy, perhaps say, "Make sure you listen to me—if I tell you to break, then break. I'm the boss in there."

"Did you go to Abraham's locker room first?" Virg asked Pabon.

"What does it matter?" the ref responded.

"Because it sounds like you had something on your mind when you came in here."

When the fight began, every time I got inside and touched Abraham, Pabon would come rushing in and yell, "Break!" This referee was determined to not let me fight on the inside that night. I got so frustrated that around the third round I said to the ref, "Let me work!" That's something I never do, but I felt it was blatantly obvious what he was doing—protecting Abraham.

Abraham stung me in the first round with a jab. *Boom! Whoa, this dude can hit,* I thought. *I can't get hit like that again.* This was the same guy who knocked Jermain Taylor out cold and beat Edison Miranda while breaking his jaw in the fourth round of their fight. I had to stay alert and focus on outboxing Abraham because the ref wouldn't let me get any work done on the inside. After the fourth round, I took command of the fight, using my speed, defense, and jab to keep Abraham at bay and frustrate him. I think if I had been allowed to fight inside the way I wanted, I would have stopped Abraham. He did not know how to defend himself, nor was he trained to fight on the inside, but I never got the chance. I won in a wide unanimous decision.

I traveled to Atlantic City to watch the other semifinal match between Englishman Carl Froch and Jamaican Glen Johnson. Deep down I didn't want to fight Johnson, another rough veteran who had nothing to lose. Froch ended up beating Johnson in a decision, setting the stage for us to meet in the Super Six final, which would take place back in Atlantic City.

I had a great camp going into the fight. But about ten days out, while I was training in Atlantic City, I threw a punch the wrong way with my left hand during my last sparring session before the fight. I felt a sharp pain shoot through my hand; I immediately knew something was wrong. When I got back to my hotel room, my hand was starting to swell profusely. My team called the New Jersey Athletic Commission to see if there were any painkillers or anti-inflammatories I could take. They wouldn't let me take anything. The next day my hand was twice its normal size when I woke up, so we went to the local ER. Unbeknownst to me, after I got an X-ray, Virg pulled the doctor aside and told him, "Don't tell him the results. Tell me."

The doctor came back and said to me that I had a "bad contusion." But he shared the real diagnosis with Virg, which was that my hand was actually fractured. This was Virg's way of trying to keep me in the right frame of mind a few days before the fight. When I heard it was just a bruise, a part of me felt a sense of relief that we were good to go, but deep down I knew my hand still didn't feel right. *This feels like something is broken,* I thought. The next couple of days were torturous for me. My hand was still swollen; I was getting ready for the biggest fight of my life, and I didn't have all my weapons. I couldn't punch with my left hand the way I wanted to and I was going in there against a world champion who was hungry to beat me.

On fight day, we wrapped my hand as tight as possible with gauze. But in the first couple of rounds, when I cracked Froch on the top of his hard head, I felt a shooting pain in my hand. The adrenaline helped me deal with the excruciating pain, but I still struggled to stay focused at times. Froch was a tough fighter, and he was hungry to win. I didn't throw nearly as many left hands as I wanted in that fight. Froch picked up the pace and made things interesting late in the fight. Afterward, people speculated that I was tired, but in reality I was trying to manage the pain in my hand. However, I still dominated most of the match. Many of my East Coast guys from Philly, New York, and DC came out to show support. It was *loud* in that arena.

I won a unanimous decision, 115–113, 115–113, 118–110. "It's a brilliant performance by Andre Ward at every level," Al Bernstein, the Hall of Fame announcer, proclaimed on Showtime after the final bell. But at one point during the fight, Froch had gotten so frustrated that he *bit* me on the shoulder. I guess referee Steve Smoger didn't see it, because when I looked at him and said, "He bit me!" he responded with, "Keep fighting!" He didn't take out a chunk of me like Tyson did to Evander Holyfield, but later that night we went to the emergency room to check on the bite and make sure it wasn't infected. At the post-fight press conference, I came in just as Froch was finishing. As he walked by, he leaned in and said, "Sorry, man, for biting you. I apologize."

"It's all good, bro," I responded.

Out of respect I did not break the code by telling the media. I didn't call him out—until a few years later, when Froch started talking too much about him losing the fight. At that point, he needed to quiet down.

FOURTEEN

STAND FOR SOMETHING

My wife and I were at home watching the Bernard Hopkins–Chad Dawson fight on HBO. I was surprised when Dawson mentioned my name during his post-fight interview with Max Kellerman. When Kellerman asked Dawson who he wanted to fight next, Dawson made a big mistake by letting his promoter, Gary Shaw, and the endorphins he was feeling convince him to call me out.

"I would love a fight with Andre Ward. It could be at 168 or 175, it doesn't matter to me," Dawson said.

I leaned forward on the couch, smiling from what I had just heard. Me and Chad were not close, but there was a mutual respect between us. I liked Chad, and he was a great fighter. I had been to several of his fights, but he was not a fighter on my radar at the time, nor did I think I was on his.

I immediately got on the phone with my manager.

"You heard that?" Prince asked.

"Yeah, I heard it," I said.

"What do you think?" he said. "I think we get him."

"Look, he said he wouldn't mind fighting at 168, let's hold him to that," I told Prince.

"You already know," Prince said. "We're on the same page."

Chad was already negotiating against himself live on national television. In negotiations, Chad and his team said they were willing to come to Oakland to challenge me for my super middleweight title. We held him to that. We didn't budge on anything.

Nine months after I beat Froch, Dawson came to town to fight me at Oracle Arena in Oakland for the super middleweight championship.

I had a lot of respect for Dawson's fight game and how he went about his career. He always seemed to want to fight the best. I was cut from that cloth, so I knew what type of fighter he was. We had to bring our best against Dawson; if he got comfortable he could beat most guys in the sport and would make them look bad in the process. My camp knew that Dawson was going to suffer by losing an extra seven pounds to make the 168-pound limit. Dawson carried around a big frame at six foot one and had been a light heavyweight for many years. It was a huge mistake for him to shock his body by losing an exorbitant amount of weight and expect to perform at the highest level. That being said, it was Dawson's misstep; we had a fight to get ready for. We had a great training camp for this fight, both mentally and physically. Everything was on point. However, we had trouble finding sparring partners who resembled Dawson's style, size, and ability. Ultimately, I had ten different guys come into camp for this fight, and most got sent home because they could not stand the heat. Whenever a sparring partner didn't perform in camp and was no longer giving me good work, Virg would send them home.

Three weeks before the fight Virg got a call from Prince. We knew Dawson had been training in Las Vegas, and my team had their eyes and ears to the streets. Similar to my training camp for the Kessler fight, we had a lot of knowledge of what Dawson was doing and how he was looking in camp. We even knew the days that Chad took off from the gym. Virg called me and said, "Dawson got knocked down and was hurt badly in sparring by Edison Miranda. Miranda cracked him with a right hand and they had to stop the sparring session."

"Are you serious?" I asked. I couldn't believe it. "Is the fight going to get canceled?"

"No, his team is just trying to keep everything under wraps until fight time. Dre, we need to stay focused—don't let this distract you," Virg said.

"I got you," I told him.

As we headed into fight week, I was shocked that the news about Dawson didn't get out. Boxing is a small business where secrets don't last very long, but this one did. I never uttered a word to the media either. I waited until the day before the fight for an opportunity to let Dawson know that I was aware of what happened to him. I wanted him to think about that over the next twenty-four hours before he stepped in the ring with me. I knew it was going to mentally drain him even more.

We both stepped off of the scale at the weigh-in; we turned toward one another face-to-face. You could hear both of our teams yelling back and forth, but I never took my eyes off of Dawson. I slowly leaned in and whispered, "I heard what happened to you in training camp. You better tighten it up tomorrow night." Checkmate. I leaned back so I could see him process what I had just said; his eyes grew big, and his shoulders slumped. It looked like all the life had left his body. He had a look on his face as if to say, *You knew this whole time?* I broke eye contact and gestured to the crowd with my fist in the air. My job was done; I had just secured victory. All I needed to do was show up and execute the game plan on fight night.

The next night the crowd was electrifying, and Dawson came ready. He was a sharpshooter with his punches: good power and good defense. But I rose to the occasion that night. I outboxed Dawson from the outside and roughed him up on the inside. My inside fighting was the difference maker in this fight. Fighting in close quarters was not something Dawson had perfected, and I took full advantage.

I knocked Dawson down three times. After the final knockdown in the tenth round, he dropped to one knee after I hit him with another combination, each punch landing flush. Dawson told referee Steve Smoger, "I'm done. I'm done." Smoger is a great referee who's not quick to stop a fight, but in this case, he had no choice. He waved his hands, signaling the fight was over. Oracle Arena erupted; the place went crazy.

"The performance from Ward was staggering. Potential-all-time-great staggering," an ESPN senior writer wrote after the fight. "This was as good as Roy Jones Jr. routing James Toney, or Floyd Mayweather Jr. crushing Diego Corrales." After winning the Super Six and then coming right back and beating the best light heavyweight in the world, I felt that I had done enough to be a first-ballot Hall of Famer. To this day I still have a lot of respect for Chad Dawson. He was a great fighter and took a huge risk coming down in weight and being willing to come to Oakland. Dawson never really rebounded after our fight, and I feel guilty about that to this day. He never should have conceded those terms for our fight at that point in his career. He didn't need to fight me, especially in my weight class. Dawson got knocked out in his next fight against Adonis Stevenson. I commentated that fight on HBO, and as I sat ringside, I felt partly responsible—I wish Dawson had never called my name. I would have been perfectly content if we had never fought.

What happened to Dawson was one of my biggest fears coming

into the sport: giving a promoter or manager too much control, which strips away a fighter's autonomy in the process. Fighters stop thinking for themselves while blindly trusting their team with career-altering decisions. This ultimately stunts the fighters' growth, keeping them utterly dependent on someone else.

This was never the vision for my career, which is why I would periodically read through my contracts to continue educating myself and make sure I was getting all that I was owed. My decision to sign with Prince under his terms, without having it vetted by an attorney, was causing me to grow discontent, and I knew I couldn't keep quiet. One of the biggest issues for me was the amount of time Prince would have me under the current contract. I started broaching the topic of the contract with him. I've never had a problem speaking truth to power, and no matter Prince's reputation, I've never feared him. I only respected him. The first conversation we had was in Houston, driving around the city.

"J, I'm looking at this contract, and I believe our contract is up." I said. "With a personal service contract in California, the maximum time it lasts is seven years."

"Oh, that's not a California contract," he said. "I gotta check, but I don't think that's in Texas law."

"Yeah, but J, you know I'm a California resident. I'm starting to feel like you have your foot on my neck."

"Oh yeah?" Prince said as he chuckled. "Why would you say that?"

"I live in California. With taxes, my check is almost cut in half before I even see it. I've outgrown this contract; I want a new deal."

He brought up the injuries that froze the contract for a little time here and there. But I had an answer for each one of his rebuttals.

Prince called me the next week. "I'm looking at this contract, Dre. It's valid."

I strongly disagreed. My wife was right. I should have never signed that initial deal under those terms.

That was the first time I brought my contract up to him. I never had to worry about Prince stealing money from me. However, he is very shrewd. You better know how to play the game, because he's not going to take it easy on you.

We would have periodic conversations about my contract. I don't think Prince realized how frustrated I was becoming and how urgent this contract situation was for me. I started to feel like Prince wasn't taking me seriously.

Prince and I had one last conversation before things took a hard left turn. We went back and forth on the phone. Then he said something that sealed it for me: "Man, you gotta do what you gotta do." I took that to mean he was done talking about it. He says he doesn't recall saying that to me. But when I heard those words, I had no choice but to take the next step.

"Alright, J," I answered.

When I hung up, I immediately called my lawyer, explained to him what happened, and let him know that we were going to have to sue Prince.

The next call was to my pastor, Napoleon Kaufman, a former NFL running back for the Oakland Raiders who was a great source of strength and counsel for me. "I'm gonna need your support with this," I told him. "Just pray for me."

He assured me that he would.

This was my first lawsuit, but deep down I knew I had to do it. I had to insist on getting my respect at the business table, not just in the ring. When the suit was filed, I was anxious—I had never done anything like this before. *I was getting ready to hit the OG!* But I knew I was standing on what was right. I trusted that God would keep me and lead me through this storm, but I knew it wasn't going to be easy. I was ready for whatever was coming.

Shortly after Prince was served with the lawsuit, I knew he would be reaching out to me. One night, at about 1:30 a.m., my phone rang. It was a private caller. I knew it was Prince. I picked up the phone.

"Hello?"

"Yeah," the voice said on the other end.

"Who is this?" I said, but I knew who it was.

"They call me James Prince," he answered.

Here we go. "What's up, J?"

"I got served with some papers from you. What is this about?"

I hadn't given him a heads-up, so I know he was shocked. "J, I've been telling you that this contract isn't right. When we talked the other day, you told me that I needed to do what I have to do, so I did."

"I don't remember saying nothing like that," he said.

"J, I'm not going to sue you just to sue you. I can't keep fighting under these terms."

Of course, Prince pushed back—he's a warrior too; he wasn't going to fold very easily.

"J, I tried to talk to you but you left me no choice. You put me in this position. This was the only way I could get you to hear me and get my respect."

I had his attention now. "Oh, I see," he said. "Now I have to get with my lawyers and see how I'm going to respond to this. I'm getting ready to countersue."

Not long after our conversation, I got served with his countersuit. I had purposely filed my lawsuit in the superior court in Oakland in an attempt to keep it out of the press. If I filed in LA, the likelihood of our suit becoming public was much higher. The lawsuits never became public knowledge.

Because of our dispute, my boxing career was now at a standstill. I had to tell my promoter that I couldn't engage in any negotiation because Prince was my representative.

Several months went by. Prince was trying to get the lawsuit changed to a Texas jurisdiction. I needed the lawsuit to stay in California, as the laws there were much stricter and favored me.

In the middle of our court battle, Prince reached out to me with a proposition. He broached the notion of us having a meeting together along with our pastors.

"We aren't making any money this way," he said. "You know I feel strong about my position, Dre. But I respect the fact that you feel strong about yours. I talked to my pastor. We thought about flying to Oakland and sitting down with you and your pastor to see what can be worked out."

Pastor Napoleon agreed to be a part of the meeting, so we invited Prince and his pastor up to the Bay Area. They pulled up to the church in a black SUV. We made our way to Pastor Napoleon's office; Prince's pastor, Ralph Douglas West, stepped out and went into the sanctuary, leaving the three of us in the office. Pastor Napoleon pulled out a notepad as Prince and I sat across from him on the other side of his desk.

"I'm happy you both are here," Pastor Napoleon said. "I know you two are going through a situation right now, and I just want to hear both sides."

I began to lay out the situation from my perspective. My pastor took notes while I spoke. Prince followed up with his perspective on how we got to this point. We talked through the percentages and the other terms of the contract that were a point of contention.

In the end, instead of doing an entirely new deal, we agreed to lower Prince's percentage. No new money was brought to the table, but I got some relief and got Prince out of my pocket a little bit. We shook hands. That was it—we both dropped our lawsuits.

I wasn't fully content, but I've since learned that a good negotiation is when neither party leaves completely satisfied.

When we ultimately did get around to talking about the lawsuit after everything was settled, Prince said, "I couldn't believe you sued me. I told myself, 'Man, Dre is cold blooded.'"

"J, you expect me to be around you as long as I have and not use some of your tactics against you?"

He fell out of his chair laughing.

Prince actually wrote about the episode in his book, *The Art and Science of Respect*, saying that he initially saw my lawsuit as a sign of disrespect, but that later "I understood then that Andre wasn't trying to cut me out or disrespect what we built together. He was trying to take control of his own destiny, and I could respect that."

That's all I've ever wanted—to have a seat at the table and be respected while I'm there. In the sport of boxing, managers and promoters expect fighters to crave money, attention, and championship belts only, but they don't expect a fighter to require respect as a business-person. We have to fight narratives and stereotypes that have been around for as long as the sport itself. "Fighters are dumb," "fighters are uneducated," "they don't read contracts," and on and on. The sad part is that those narratives are not completely false, but I have never appreciated the way fighters are viewed. By the grace of God, this didn't happen to me. I pushed back. I asked questions. I forced my team to earn their money. I wanted to beat the sport more than any other opponent.

After the Dawson fight, I was scheduled to fight former middleweight champ Kelly Pavlik in Los Angeles in January 2013. Pavlik still had a strong name in the sport; this was going to be a big one for me, but an old injury that had been haunting me since I was a kid reappeared, which put a whole lot of things in doubt.

When I was twelve years old, I tore my right rotator cuff in an amateur fight against one of my rivals, Joaquin Marquez. The doctor said I was too young to have surgery. We were told that I should just do some rehab and things would get better. Years later, we found out that I did need surgery.

Over the years I would continue to do extensive rehab on my shoulder. It became a part of my training regimen, doing whatever I could to strengthen my rotator cuff. My shoulder *was* getting incrementally better, but it was far from full strength and was very unstable, which made me hesitant to even want to throw it. It always felt like it was on the verge of popping out. Though it was frustrating not having all my weapons, I learned to compensate by using my right hand for defense and making my left hand even greater. What's interesting is that over the years no one outside of my team recognized that I had a shoulder issue or that I rarely threw my right hand. I was essentially a one-handed fighter for most of my career. There were times when I could put the injury out of my mind and other times my deficiencies consumed me. My focus was on what I did not possess instead of what I was able to accomplish even with my injury.

In my personal time with God, I would ask him, "Why can't I have two good arms?" I would daydream about what type of fighter I could be if only my right shoulder were healthy. I realized that God was less concerned about healing my shoulder and more concerned about teaching me to be utterly dependent on him. As I read the Word (the Bible), I would feel God speaking to me. For example, 2 Corinthians 12:9 reads, "My grace is sufficient for you, for My strength is made perfect in weakness." This is the story of my life. This passage speaks about how the apostle Paul had a thorn in his flesh. He pleaded with the Lord to remove the thorn and the hardship—but the Lord essentially answered Paul by saying, "Your weaknesses and your deficiencies won't stop you, for my strength and my power will be enough even when you are weak." I wasn't suffering for Jesus like the apostle Paul, but I could relate. Even though I didn't have a normal shoulder and things weren't perfect, God was telling me to trust him more and that his grace and help would be sufficient.

Dr. Michael Dillingham, a former orthopedic surgeon for the San Francisco 49ers, eventually opened up my shoulder in 2013. He saw that the subscapularis—which is responsible for about 50 percent of the strength in a shoulder—was just hanging there unattached. It had likely been hanging there since I was twelve; I just didn't know it. The good news was that the nerves were still attached to the subscapularis; it hadn't atrophied, but it wasn't connected. That meant it wasn't providing any protection to my shoulder capsule, which allowed the capsule to tear.

Dillingham was shocked that I had boxed as long as I had without any major issues. "How often does your shoulder pop out of the socket?" he asked.

"Never, it only feels like it's going to pop out," I said. It was only when I was getting ready for the Pavlik fight that the shoulder finally gave way.

"We're going to have to do surgery," the doctor said.

"You have to do what?"

I couldn't believe it. It was going to be a complicated surgery that could end my career if it didn't go right. Suddenly, a lot of the agony I had gone through over the past sixteen years made sense. From the age of twelve to twenty-eight, I struggled with being a one-handed fighter. Everything that I had accomplished, from the Olympics to the Super

Six, I had done with my left hand. As a result, my left hand became lethal. Because of my shoulder problems, I had had to elevate my skill level and my ring IQ. I'd had to use my brain to find a way around it. I'd learned to overcompensate, and what I did not possess in one area resulted in other areas of my fight game becoming elite.

This process came with anguish and struggle. There were times when I would be in tears, angry and frustrated about my condition, comparing myself to other fighters. During these moments, Virg would console me, tell me to let it go.

"Listen, Dre. God is allowing this to happen to you. You have to learn to trust him," Virg said. "The purpose of this is so you don't think you're doing this in your own strength; God is keeping you humble."

Virg was always working on my mind and speaking to my spirit. He knew that we had to look beyond boxing for my purpose. My dad gave me a foundation in faith, and Virg took the baton and kept the purpose of God very much in the forefront of my mind. It was always a spiritual battle to me, not just a physical one. His words were encouraging because I would have moments where I felt like my shoulder injury wasn't fair. But when I looked at the results, I couldn't complain because I kept winning. The thorn in my side ultimately did keep me humble because I knew that my success came from hard work but ultimately the grace of God on my life. *Dude, you won most of your fights with one arm.* This was deeper than an injury to me; it was a metaphor for my life. God has always given me much, but not so much to where I didn't need him.

"I haven't seen anybody beat you in a long time," he continued. "Maybe he doesn't want you to have two good arms. Maybe he thinks you just need one because he can do more with less."

In the years before my surgery, Virg would tell me, "God is going to heal that shoulder one day." I didn't really believe him. Well, a part of me did, because he had always been prophetically accurate with a lot of things in my life.

The night before the surgery, I went to Dillingham's San Francisco home. I listened to him describe the entire procedure one last time and answer any lingering questions I had. As I sat in the living room, I felt the presence of God. My eyes welled with tears.

"God's going to heal my shoulder," I told the doctor. "I can feel it."

The doctor nodded, unsure of what to say next. But I felt compelled to express that—I think more for me than for him.

It was such a delicate procedure. If they struck the wrong nerve, it could have ended my career. I could have permanently lost feeling in my right arm. Dr. Dillingham had an all-star team of surgeons from the Bay Area working with him to fix my shoulder.

When I woke up from surgery, the first thing I said was, "Doc, did you get it? My subscapularis."

He nodded. "We got it."

But he wasn't ready yet to say the surgery was a success. Dillingham is honest like that, which I why I will always love Dr. D. "I don't say that it's successful until you're able to get back to doing what you were doing, or doing it better," he said.

When it came time for rehab, Dillingham's partner Lisa Giannone, who's a world-class physical therapist, took over. I thank God for this woman because I needed her at that time. She's petite, but she's aggressive and doesn't take any mess. Lisa's going to tell you the truth without holding anything back. Rehabbing the shoulder was an incremental process. The surgery successfully reattached the subscapularis, but that was no guarantee the shoulder would work properly, I would have full movement, or my body would respond well. Some days I would show up to rehab and tell Lisa that something didn't feel right in my shoulder that day.

"Oh, you've got the black cloud today," she said the first time that happened.

She wouldn't even entertain my worries. She was always ready to get to work. She'd just keep pressing and pressing. When we finally got through it months later, I definitely came out better on the other side. It still wasn't 100 percent yet, but my shoulder was stronger, more powerful. I had more trust and faith in its ability. This was the best my shoulder had felt since I was twelve years old.

After a fourteen-month absence and nine months of intense physical therapy, it was time for me to test my shoulder in a boxing ring. On November 16, 2013, I fought the number one ranked super middleweight contender, Edwin Rodríguez.

I had missed being in my element, dealing with the pressure, expectations, and everything that came with professional prizefighting. It was not lost on me that there would be no soft spot for me to fall if I failed in this fight with Rodríguez. Even though I'd been off for fourteen months, many wanted to see if I could pick up where I left off. I was okay with that because those were my expectations too.

I felt good in the fight. I was in great shape, eager for my return, and I performed well. I won the fight by a wide margin after twelve rounds, and showed the world that I was back. When I rewatched the fight, I still wasn't using my right hand that much and was still heavily dependent on my left hand. My team of doctors and physical therapists said that was normal and over time I would be comfortable throwing the right hand again. They were right. Dr. D and Lisa were ringside, and they were pleased with what they saw.

The lonely nine months that I spent in rehab, grinding to get back, spoke loudly to me. My phone wasn't ringing, nor did I get a lot of attention in that season. I realized I wasn't making money for anyone and therefore I wasn't a priority. But the fighting brought back the limelight and brought back the crowd. These times in my life always help me keep attention and fame in their proper place. I realized that I was a commodity to many, and this was a business and I needed to treat it as such.

It's been well publicized that my promoter Dan Goossen and I had a business rift. We just were not seeing eye to eye on some very important issues. Ultimately, I chose to file a lawsuit against Dan Goossen and Goossen Tutor Promotions and the legal battle took nearly two years.

Dan is not here to tell his side nor to speak his piece about this matter so I will refrain from going into any significant detail. There's been a lot said about the lawsuit period in my career that questioned my motives and integrity and was blatantly false and inaccurate. At this point in my life, I don't have the time nor energy to try to correct false narratives anymore. Neither of our legacies are defined by this period. Ironically, we were both inducted into the International Boxing Hall of Fame on the same weekend.

At one point in time, Dan Goossen and I were like family, and sometimes family fights. Unfortunately for us, our fight was public. Dan passed in the middle of our dispute, so both sides will forever be without closure.

During this period, I gained wisdom and drew a lot of strength from Bernard Hopkins. Throughout the years, I talked to B-Hop and would pick his brain about the business of boxing and more specifically how to navigate litigation with my promoter. He told me what to expect and encouraged me that I was doing the right thing. Hopkins said I needed to stand up for what I believed in. He had come from nothing and achieved great things. "If you don't stand up for yourself in this sport, no one will stand up for you," he told me.

Taking this stand was not popular, and it was a very lonely period.

The phone stopped ringing. I'm grateful for the ones close to me that stayed in touch to keep me encouraged. The truth is that the number of people who check on you when things are good does not equal the number who check on you during times of turmoil.

I thought back to every surgery that I'd undergone. It would only be me and my wife and sometimes Virg at 4:30 in the morning as I was strapped to an IV and praying that everything would turn out alright. I would look around and wonder, *Where's everybody at?* No one was obligated to show up, but this gave me perspective. Every decision that I made in the sport needed to benefit me and my family over everyone else.

I grappled with similar thoughts during the legal battle. The media continued to clamor for me to talk, but I was limited on what I could say because I didn't want to jeopardize my case. There were many headlines and reports that were simply untrue: "Ward would rather fight in the courtroom than fight in the ring." *This makes no sense. There's money going out but no money coming in. I've got three kids and a mortgage.* I was fighting for something bigger than what the media could see. I wasn't conforming and doing what they thought was best for my career, so I stood out as the outlier, and this was the only way they knew how to respond.

People have wondered for years why professional athletes go broke. There are many reasons. Many come from nothing, and financial literacy is not easy to learn or to execute. When you come into money for the first time, your natural inclination is *What can I buy?* Most people aren't taught about stocks, bonds, exchange-traded funds (ETFs), or real estate. Education about pension plans or 401(k)s is scarce. It's not about what you make or even how much you save but how you invest.

Things are a little different for athletes in leagues like the NFL and the NBA. They have access to financial literacy courses when they get drafted. The players' unions look out for their short- and long-term interests, but we don't have that in boxing, and it doesn't seem like the powers that be want that to change.

I didn't have formal financial training, but business has always intrigued me, which led to much research and many questions of those around me who had more experience in this space. My wife and I realized very early on that having long-term financial success would come from saving, budgeting, and investing our money. This paid dividends during the lean times of the lawsuit. Because we were living below our means, we didn't have to borrow money from my manager or anyone else. My kids didn't miss any meals, and all of our bills were paid. We were able to fight this fight with a clear mind without the worry of money influencing our decisions. Even though I was uncomfortable in this storm, I never had to panic.

As the legal battle dragged on, I heard that a young film director, Ryan Coogler, an Oakland native, was trying to get in touch with me, but I didn't really think much about it. What could a director want with me? One day, Ryan called me.

"Hey bro, it's good to talk to you," he said. "I've been supporting you throughout your career."

As we talked, it became clear to me that he knew a lot about me. I didn't know as much about him, other than the fact that he'd directed *Fruitvale Station*, a movie about the 2009 killing of Oscar Grant by the BART police in Oakland. That incident happened a few blocks from the gym where I trained, King's Gym. The film had been widely acclaimed, but I hadn't seen it.

"I want to come meet you," he said. "I've got a role for you."

"A role?" I repeated. "A role for what?"

"I've got this boxing movie. It's gonna be a spinoff of the *Rocky* franchise."

He gave me an overview of the storyline. It sounded interesting, so I agreed to meet with him. He came out to meet me and we sat down and talked at a restaurant. He laid out the plot for *Creed* and what my role would be. I thought, *This is crazy. I've never acted in a movie before, and he doesn't really know me like that, but he's asking me to be a part of this movie?*

From what I heard that day, it sounded dope; it was something I could see myself doing. I try not to make decisions just based on money or opportunity alone. I weigh every decision that I make through prayer and counsel. Ryan sent me the early script to help me in my decision-making process, which is not something that's usually done for someone who's never acted before, but that's just how Ryan is. It was a couple hundred pages long. I started skimming through it and saw a lot of vulgarity and a few sex scenes that made me pause. *Man, I don't think I can do this.* I talked to my wife, shared my concerns, and told her how I felt.

"Are you sure?" she asked.

The next day I called Ryan and explained to him where I was at. "Ryan, I appreciate you giving me this opportunity, but I'm not sure I can do it."

"What do you mean?" Ryan said.

"There's more language than I expected and a few scenes that I'm not comfortable with, and you know I don't get down like that," I told him.

"Listen, Dre," he said. "The script is written like that for emphasis. This is a PG-13 film, and you can only have a certain amount of cuss words, and those other scenes will be taken out." That made sense to me. I told Ryan we'd talk in a few weeks, and I hung up the phone.

The next time I talked to Ryan, he had some reinforcements; he had Michael B. Jordan on three-way. We had a similar conversation as the first but a little bit more detailed this time, which gave me more understanding about the overall script and put me at ease.

"Trust me," Ryan said. "I know how you get down, and I respect it. I'm not going to put you in that position. The *Rocky* franchise isn't gonna let us say certain things in this movie. There's a certain fan base they have."

I agreed to do it, playing the role of Danny "Stuntman" Wheeler, and I'm glad I did. It was one of the greatest experiences in my life. My respect grew for Michael B. and Ryan because in the preproduction phase, they invested the time to come out to my gym in the Bay Area. They immersed themselves in the sport of boxing. They asked all the right questions, and me and Virg gave them as much knowledge as we could.

They wanted to get it right, and it showed in the final product. When it came time to head to Philly for the actual filming, there were stuntmen there teaching fighters how to fall properly and even how to throw punches for the camera. My sparring scene was choreographed, so I had stuntmen working with me on every punch.

I felt like I had to undo everything I'd been taught and relearn how to throw punches to make it look cinematic.

When the movie came out, I couldn't believe how much it blew up. I run into people all over the world, and to this day, some don't know I'm a real fighter. They just know me from *Creed*.

In the middle of all my legal drama, this was a healthy distraction that I needed to keep my mind off of everything else I was dealing with. As I continued to sit and wait for the court proceedings to play out, I would often call my pastor in moments of anxiety.

"Pastor, do you think I'm done? Do you think this is it? Maybe God wants me to be done fighting."

He started laughing. "Absolutely not!"

"Pastor, listen," I said. "Do you see what's happening right now?"

"Dre, listen. God still has to get more glory out of your life. This isn't it. I don't know exactly what's going to happen, but this too shall pass."

Those phone calls were faith injections for me. I still had to battle moments of doubt because the optics didn't look good. Between the ongoing court battles, the headlines that I was reading, and the time I was losing in my career, I felt like it was time to write a retirement speech and send it out. My thinking was that if I was going to go out, I was going out on my own terms. I shared my thoughts with my wife and she was immediately against it.

"Don't do it," she said. "It's premature. Don't do it. Just hang in there."

I continued to participate in all the calls with the lawyers regarding my lawsuit. I couldn't put my life and career in somebody else's hands. We had already tried to settle the lawsuit multiple times, but we continued to get shot down.

I was at home when I got the call from Prince that Goossen had died. He'd had stage-four liver cancer. I was extremely hurt because I had love for Dan. We took a chance on each other coming out of the Olympics. He took me from a gold medal to multiple world championships, and for that, I will forever be grateful. The hardest part about his passing for me is that there will never be any closure.

I wanted to attend the funeral and pay my respects, but I didn't feel it would be appropriate with how things ended. Prince pressed his way in and went and paid his respects on behalf of the team.

Ultimately, we were able to settle my lawsuit with the Goossen family. Once the paperwork was finalized, I became a free agent for the first time since 2004, which made way for a conversation with Jay-Z and Roc Nation.

They had just started a boxing division, which I thought was interesting. This was exactly what I was looking for. I was either going to promote myself or sign with a company that brought something new and fresh to the game. After everything I had just gone through, I was looking for more of a partnership and more control, and Roc Nation gave me that opportunity.

I knew this deal with Roc Nation would likely be my last, so I wanted to get it right. Desiree and Juan Perez, CEO of Roc Nation and president of Roc Nation Sports, respectively, were shrewd, but with all my years in the boxing game and my time dealing with Prince, I was ready. There was the obvious back-and-forth with each side fighting to keep as much as possible and give as little as possible. That's the nature of a big negotiation. I knew I couldn't get everything I wanted, but that didn't stop me from fighting for it.

I was ready for a new chapter. We announced the deal on my social media channels with a picture of me and Jay-Z sitting at a table. I think we broke the internet that day. There was a lot of excitement from media and fans after so many had written me off. The next three years would be the most lucrative of my career and would ultimately seal my fate as a first-ballot Hall of Famer.

FIFTEEN

KRUSHER

The next big question was: Who will I fight next?

HBO had a lot to say about that; they wanted me to move up to light heavyweight and fight the reigning light heavyweight champion, Sergey Kovalev. It was hard to avoid HBO's giant footprint. They paid the most money, had the biggest audience, and had the best fighters and the best fights. I was under contract with HBO, which meant they would suggest multiple opponents for me to fight and we would pick one.

But I wasn't ready to move up to a higher weight class at that time. It was a bit challenging for me to get down to 168, but I felt like it was still comfortable enough for me stay there. I still had a few more fights in me at 168 pounds and felt I had earned the right to choose when I wanted to go up. But HBO was looking for the fights that would make them the most money and attract the most eyeballs, so they were trying to force my hand and make me move up. We presented a list of opponents who were viable options at super middleweight, but they weren't budging. Eventually the conversation would shift back to fighting Kovalev. He was the truth, a fighter who had earned every bit of his reputation and who had killed a man in the ring five years earlier. He knocked out fellow Russian Roman Simakov so viciously that the twenty-seven-year-old never regained consciousness and died three days later from brain injuries. Kovalev's nickname was "Krusher," and the name fit—the man could crack. He was known for going to other fighters' home countries and knocking them out. He was physically big and he was mean.

Throughout my career I had fought everybody who'd been put in front of me; I never ducked a soul. I did not appreciate the way I was being handled by HBO. The network only gave us one option: move up to a higher class in my next fight and take on arguably the most feared guy in the sport. I'd been loyal to HBO—I'd fought and commentated for them. This was another reminder that boxing was still very much a business.

I had to step back and process what my next move was going to be. *I'm a fighter, and I'm not turning down a fight.* But my business mind stepped in and said, *Dre, this is prizefighting, not pride fighting.* That's what Virg would always tell me. I had to put my pride aside so I could think clearly. I read comments that Floyd Mayweather made about the potential fight with me and Kovalev—the rumblings about the fight had been leaked by now.

"Yeah, they're setting Ward up," he said. "It's a setup. Why should he have to go to 175 to fight this dude instead of staying at 168?"

Throughout my career, I felt like Floyd respected me, but he never really embraced me. Anytime we were face-to-face, Floyd would extend his hand and there would be mutual respect, but that's really where it ended. Most of the time Floyd had something to say about me publicly, it was negative or a backhanded compliment. I don't fully know why;

that's something only he can answer. But deep down I knew he was right about this one. This felt different; I felt like I was being pushed into a new weight class and this fight against Kovalev, even after a long hiatus due to the lawsuit.

I was at another crossroads, and I didn't know which way to go, so I prayed on it. If I walked away from this, I didn't know when I would fight again. I had only fought twice in the last three years; I couldn't afford another setback, and I wanted to start the Roc Nation relationship the right way.

I'd learned to take my time when making these sorts of decisions. I would always be slow to respond to my team because if I made the wrong decision, ultimately it would fall on me. I'd learned to measure twice and cut once. As a younger fighter, I used to be overly concerned with what the network or my team thought when it was time to pick an opponent or make a decision like this. But as I grew up in the sport, I learned to weigh those opinions, and ultimately, I had the final say. The way I do business is the way I fight. I think my way through.

The opponent I would face played a big part in my thought process. When facing a fighter of that level, you have to have your mind right. He had never been beaten. He had crazy power. I believed I could beat him, but I knew it wasn't going to be easy.

All of that was on my mind when I woke up one Sunday morning and got ready for church. Like I typically do in these situations, I spoke to God, looking for direction.

During decision-making times like these, my wife will typically give me room to go through my process, but she will always find ways to give me the right words at the right time. My wife is a very wise woman, and she isn't a scary lady; she's got some dog in her. She was disappointed that HBO didn't treat us better. But like always, she fell back on the same position: let's pray and see what God says.

One of the ministers of our church preached a message that morning called "Who, Me? Couldn't Be." He spoke of God picking Gideon and choosing him to go to war against the Midianites to save Israel even though Israel was grossly outnumbered. God told Gideon that although the deck was stacked against him, God was with him and it would be enough. I listened intently to that message; it spoke directly to me. I went down to the altar afterward, got down on my knees, and prayed. One of the elders came up and prayed with me as if reading my mind.

"God, lead him and guide him. Remind him that you're with him and that no weapon formed against him shall prosper." *Boom*, that was it. There might be weapons forming around me, but they would not prosper.

It has never ceased to amaze me throughout my career and personal life how God speaks to me and leads me through these situations once I have acknowledged that I need his direction. It is not an audible voice but a feeling deep in my spirit, and I know that God is leading me in a certain direction. This is how my faith, life, and career intersect. When I left the church that day, my perspective was different. It shifted from being too concerned about what was coming against me from the business end to realizing that it wasn't going to play out the way some may have intended. That this was an opportunity, not a setup.

I called Prince the next day and said, "Let's get the fight done. I'm ready. If I'm going to take the fight, I need you to do one thing for me. I need two fights at light heavyweight before the Kovalev fight. I need to shake off some ring rust."

Even though this was the only option that HBO had given me, I still had some leverage. Contracts don't fight; fighters do. I knew HBO didn't have a lot of options for Kovalev either. They needed *me* to take this fight as much as they needed *him* to. The network wanted me to take only one fight, then jump right into the Kovalev fight, but that wasn't going to happen. I told Prince, "I will walk away from this if they don't give me two tune-up fights before Kovalev."

HBO initially protested, but finally they agreed to it. When it was announced that the Ward–Kovalev fight would take place in Las Vegas in November, you could feel the buzz right away. Some media members were calling it one of the most anticipated bouts in the last twenty-five years—the best super middleweight in the world going against the best light heavyweight in the world. Boxing has always been more enamored with power and strength than with IQ and skill. Many people were saying that perhaps I had bitten off more than I could chew. But there were others predicting that my skill set would be too much for Kovalev. In other words, it was stacking up to be a battle for the ages.

After they announced the fight, some of my insecurities began to eat away at me. We were required to start appearing at events together to build up the anticipation for the fight. HBO wanted me to go to Kovalev's fight in Montreal, Canada, against Jean Pascal.

After I landed in Montreal, I knew Kovalev and I were going to see each other face-to-face. He and the media would be sizing me up. I wanted to look the part; I needed to look like a full-fledged light heavyweight, like I belonged at this weight class. This was a mistake; my focus was off. Usually, I never worried about my appearance or looking the part. I had always been more focused on substance, getting the job done on fight night—when it matters the most. The two or three days I was there I stayed in the gym, lifting weights, doing push-ups, anything I could think of to increase my bulk. I wanted anyone who saw me to acknowledge that I belonged at this weight. Deep down, I knew that I was breaking code, but my insecurities got the best of me. Bulk was never my game—I've always been sneaky strong, and there wasn't ever a fighter in my pro career who felt stronger than me or who bullied me in a boxing ring—but I lost sight of this and forgot about what had ultimately gotten me to this point. One of my greatest assets as a fighter has always been my mind: mental toughness and resolve. Some wrongly assume that if you are mentally tough, you no longer must do the work to stay that way, or that it's impossible to lose confidence. Mental reps must be taken daily. There are times that you will have to remind yourself of who you are when doubt tries to creep in, and to reassure yourself that who you are is enough for the task at hand.

Before our fight, Kovalev always presented himself to me in a respectful way. He had this sinister confidence, a smug smile that told you he didn't have a care in the world. "Ward's a great champion, but of course I think I'm gonna knock him out!" he told the media, laughing. The thing about big punchers is that it's a gift but it can also be a curse. It's a gift because you can hit someone with one punch and the fight could be over. That thought can be intoxicating. But when a fighter falls in love with their power, they sometimes lose the desire to work on other elements of their game. That will always come back to bite them at the worst time. The world would soon find out that Kovalev fell into that second category.

I got my first glimpse into his mind at our first big press conference in New York. We had to get there a few hours early to sign gloves for sponsors and do interviews with different outlets. Whenever I would interact with an opponent, I considered it the fight *before* the fight, an opportunity to read them and to send a message: *I'm here.* I wanted them to feel my presence. I walked past Kovalev in the hallway. I looked at him directly in his eyes as he stared right back at me. We slowly walked past each other and I made it a point not to speak to or acknowledge him, and he returned the favor. Kovalev had a reputation as a bully, a guy who other fighters feared. That wasn't going to be me. Kovalev carried that Mike Tyson–like aura; he possessed power and a mean reputation, and he invoked fear. Though I respected Tyson as a fighter, I was never enamored with his approach. Since I was a young kid, I had been groomed to break down and beat that mentality, not to fear it.

I later found out how Kovalev felt about our exchange—and just as I thought, he responded exactly like a bully would. He told an interviewer that he was shocked and offended that I had walked past him without a word. He then followed that up with an expletive. He was shocked that I wasn't enamored with the fact that he was Sergey Kovalev. That one comment told me that he didn't really understand the type of mind and fighter he was getting ready to face. He didn't grasp that there are these small battles before the actual fight; for me, the first bell had already rung. I felt like I was way ahead of him with the mental warfare.

The media never embraced him as a darling, but they feared and respected him. I felt that Kovalev and his team used the fact that he killed Roman Simakov as some sort of badge of honor. That deeply offended me. I get disgusted when anybody in our sport glorifies death. As competitive as we are, that's the one thing every fighter should be praying against. I always prayed that God would help both me and my opponent get home safe. In the end, that's all that mattered.

If I'm honest, there were moments when I would stop and think about that. It would pop into my head: *That dude killed somebody.* Then I would audibly say, "But that's not going to happen to me. He's not killing anybody." I think fighters make huge mistakes by not acknowledging the good that they see in their opponent. It's a defense mechanism that gives a fighter false confidence and helps them believe they can win. But I was taught to be honest about who I was fighting. In fact, in my camp we probably gave more credit to an opponent than he deserved to ensure we were ready. When you are honest about who and what you are facing, it helps you to get up early, stay late, and do everything in your power to have the right mindset stepping into the ring.

Before Kovalev, I first fought Cuban number one light heavyweight contender Sullivan Barrera at the Oracle Arena in Oakland on March 26, 2016. I knocked him down in the third round and easily won a unanimous decision. Three months later, on June 28, I beat Colombian fighter Alexander Brand in another unanimous decision at the Oracle Arena. At the time, I didn't realize this would be the last time I would ever fight in my hometown.

The mega-fight against Kovalev was set for November 19 in Las Vegas. Oddly enough, it would be my first fight in Vegas, the boxing capital of the world.

As my preparation for the fight kicked off, I utilized one of my training secrets—Pilates. I initially started Pilates while I was still an amateur in my teens. I was resistant at first.

"Man, that's for girls," I told Virg when he suggested it. "I don't want to do Pilates!"

"Trust me," Virg said.

He educated me on the history of Pilates, which was started by a German named Joseph Pilates, who was a former professional boxer. That changed my perspective.

"Strength from the inside out is real strength," Virg said. "You need to be flexible, but you need to also have your core right."

We started going to a Pilates studio that used to be in Oakland called The Working Body, near Lake Merritt. For several years leading up to the Olympics, they let me train there for free. They supported me until I turned professional and could pay them.

In addition to Pilates, I hired the legendary Mackie Shilstone, a personal trainer renowned for helping athletes build muscle, and more specifically, helping fighters to successfully move up in weight. Mackie took both Michael Spinks and Roy Jones Jr. from the light heavyweight division to heavyweight glory. He'd also worked with elite athletes as diverse as Peyton Manning and Serena Williams. I thought, *If it worked for Roy, it'll work for me*. But Virg was against it.

"We don't need that kind of training," he told me.

I wasn't afraid that another boxer was bigger than me—that was normal—but it was the perception of others that I was too concerned with. I brought in Mackie and he did his job by building me up, and Virg wasn't happy about it.

I had one major issue that nobody knew about: my right knee. Because of a previous ACL surgery in 2008 and the amount of running and boxing training I was doing, my knee would flare up and swell significantly at times. I typically managed it with rest and a high-end ice machine called Game Ready. The problem was that I was in the middle of the most important camp of my career, getting ready for the fight of my life. Long rest periods were not an option, and the ice wasn't working.

I did not train at an average pace. I would push the limits with everything: running, jumping rope, shadowboxing, and sparring. In this camp my rhythm was constantly being disrupted and I hated it. After two good days, the knee would be in pain and I'd have to back off. Another good day and my knee would swell to the size of a grapefruit, and we would be forced to cancel my training for the next few days.

I'm a thinker. I'm constantly taking inventory of where I am in my training. *Am I doing enough? How did I look today?* At this point, with all the disruptions, the math wasn't adding up for me, and that concerned me. With three weeks left in camp, I was forced to go to my surgeon and allow him to do an MRI and an examination. He revealed there was no structural damage, which was a good thing, but said my workload was causing the swelling. My doctor drained my knee to alleviate some of the pressure. The next three weeks in camp were the hardest I've had in my career. I was physically wounded, emotionally drained, and struggling from day to day. I found myself asking God, *Why this? Why now?* With ten days left before the fight there was still a slight possibility that I might not make it to Vegas. I was on the phone with Virg, Prince, and Josh, in tears.

"I can't pull out of this fight," I said. "I already know what would be said. I can't have a setback right now. I need to fight."

I was fighting the most dangerous man I had ever faced and I was far from being 100 percent. Virg was trying to lift me up.

"You're going to be fine," he said.

"I don't know, Virg. How can I fight with one leg?"

"The same way God brought you through every other time, he's going to bring you through again."

I wanted to believe Virg; I knew in my heart he was right. I believed God was going to see me through, but it was hard to wrap my mind around the fact that I was less than two weeks away and I wasn't physically at my best. There was a war raging internally between faith, doubt, and the reality I was facing.

We weighed our options until it was time for me to leave for Las Vegas. I had to keep a poker face at the gym around the rest of my team and my sparring partners. No one knew what I was dealing with except for a few close-knit people. Anytime I spoke to the media, I had to tell them that camp was going according to schedule. There was no scenario where I could give the media the scoop about what was unfolding. That just wasn't going to happen. Historically in boxing, if a fighter pulls out of a big fight, the first thing your opponent will say is, "He's scared." Whatever your reason is—even if your mother died or you're badly hurt—it doesn't matter. I bit down and stepped out in faith.

The day before we boarded the plane to leave for Vegas, one week before the fight, I had to once again visit the doctor to have my knee drained. I watched them stick a huge needle in my knee and pull out the fluid. Doc also wanted me to wear a big knee brace in order to stabilize my knee, but I refused. I couldn't give Kovalev the confidence of me looking wounded. Whatever was going to happen to the knee was going to happen. We were trying everything we could to keep the fight from being canceled. Meanwhile, thoughts were bombarding my mind. It felt unfair, like the deck was stacked against me. What I learned from this camp is what I learned about God throughout my whole career: everything that he allows to happen to me is with purpose and ultimately working for my good. I was going to need to hold onto that truth with both hands if I was going to make it through this storm.

A few hours before I was set to leave from my rented house in Vegas to head to the arena, Dr. Dillingham was with me in the living room, draining my knee one last time. He pulled out about 4 cc of fluid. I watched in disbelief as he drained my knee. It felt surreal—was this really happening? The biggest moment of my career was waiting, and I needed to show up—not just physically but mentally and emotionally. There was no time to doubt, no time to question the circumstances I was dealing with. It was time to go to war.

As I arrived to T-Mobile Arena, my adrenaline was pumping and the knee was pushed back to the recesses of my mind. *We're here now.* I told myself there was no way God was going to put me in this position and not see me through. As I sat in the locker room, my belief and faith fed my spirit. I was fully convinced that I was in Vegas on this night with a purpose. At times it can be hard to believe that God will allow hardships to invade our lives—but he will. God did not need me to be perfect; he was looking for complete trust and for my faith to be in him, not in my own strength. On November 19, 2016, I knew I was going to have to walk through some fire.

My locker room was packed; the energy was high; there was tension in the air. An HBO producer came to my locker room in a panic: "It's time for you to walk!" I was the challenger so I was required to walk first. The champion walks second. I mentally went to a different place; I was locked in. It's an art form. As I walked through the long hallway leading to the arena, the energy and noise from the crowd got louder. The anticipation and expectation for the fight became palpable. The pressure I felt was real, but the confidence and belief I had were stronger. I belonged; I was there for a reason.

When I reached the arena floor, my music exploded through the speakers. The crowd went crazy. Fans were yelling and screaming; many were with me, but some were against me. I remembered all the conversations we'd had in training camp and all the sacrifices over the years.

As I stepped into that ring, I scanned the crowd, but the only people I ever made eye contact with were my family. I blew them a kiss and let them know Daddy was good.

I saw all the A-listers sitting ringside. When Kovalev showed up, I gave him a look that said, *It's about to go down.*

I went to a neutral corner and kneeled to pray. *God, I need you. I need you right now.* As my team was putting Vaseline on my face and we were preparing for the prefight announcement, I felt the nerves more than I ever had before. But they were controlled nerves.

When the fight began, I came out tight. I was thinking when I should have been reacting. Meanwhile, Kovalev got off to a fast start, hitting me with stiff jabs in the center of my face. As a fighter, I'm going to get hit, but not like *that*. I don't usually get hit with flush punches in the center of my face, especially in the first round. His punches didn't hurt, but they were sharp, accurate shots that I definitely felt. I was more impressed with the accuracy of his punches than I was with his power. With each punch that landed, I could hear the reaction from the crowd. I wasn't in my groove yet. My feet were stationary; I was a sitting target. I'm not sure if that was a result of my knee or my nerves. In the corner, Virg let me know I wasn't looking like myself. "You got to relax! You got to settle down!"

In the second round, with forty seconds to go before the round was over, I made a rookie mistake. I had my left hand down with my chin in the air as we exchanged right hands. Kovalev's right hand connected before mine could. *Boom!* I went down hard. This was only the second time in my career I had been knocked down. Ironically this was the eleven-year anniversary, to the day, of my first knockdown. I've heard other fighters who would describe getting hit, and without realizing it, they would be on the canvas trying to figure out how they got there. I had just experienced this feeling for the first time.

I looked up as the arena erupted. I couldn't believe it. *This dude just knocked me down.* As I looked across the ring, I could see Kovalev's sinister grin and his body language that said, *Yeah, I knew this was gonna happen,* as if him knocking me out was a foregone conclusion.

As I rose to my feet, I felt my father's fighting spirit in my veins. You hit my father with a good shot, he was gonna get angry, and he would eventually get that lick back. In a matter of seconds, I did a self-assessment. I was trying to figure out, *Am I good?* I wasn't hurt, just buzzed. I could feel my legs under me. That's what you call a flash knockdown.

My dad used to train me in our living room when I was eleven or twelve on what to do if I ever got knocked down. "Don't rush up, son. Take a second. Depending on how you fell, you roll over and get on one knee. Then give yourself a second to rise. Don't just jump up." Some guys jump up and they're not ready yet. Pride and embarrassment take over, and they don't give themselves adequate time to fully get their wits back. Within a few seconds, I went from being shocked that I had been knocked down, to being embarrassed, to now being angry.

Referee Robert Byrd came over and asked, "Are you okay?" I nodded and smiled to say to Kovalev, *Good shot, you got me—now I'm coming to get that back!*

The referee instructed us to fight. Kovalev did what he was trained to do—he moved in to finish me off. I did what I was trained to do—I slowed the pace of the fight, held, made the referee do his job until I was able to clear my head. I just needed to get back to my corner to regroup. I felt the threat was over. The bell rang; I'd gotten through that moment.

I had one of the most underrated chins in boxing. My ability to take a punch was never talked about. I've faced some of the biggest punchers in my respective weight classes, and Kovalev was one the biggest punchers in the sport of boxing. I took everything that was dished out and only left my feet twice in a thirty-two-fight career. My boxing ability and mental toughness are what are typically highlighted—but my chin was actually one of my best-kept secrets.

As I walked to my corner, I felt like I could hear what everybody in the arena was thinking: *We knew that was gonna happen—it was just a matter of time. Ward can't deal with Kovalev's power.*

When I sat down, Virg was in my ear immediately. From that point forward, he coached the best fight of his career. "Look at me! Look at me!" he yelled.

"I hear you," I responded, though I didn't look at him.

"You know what we're here for! You're great. Don't worry about a knockdown. Don't even entertain it. You understand me?"

I nodded.

Virg told me that I needed to win every round going forward—and that's pretty much what I did. I hate to admit it, but I needed that knockdown; it helped me stop overthinking and start reacting. I was so consumed with getting Kovalev back that I forgot I was in a big fight. At this point, I was just in a fight. I knew I was behind early, so I fought with a real sense of urgency. I was being forced to do something I had never had to do in my professional career: come from behind. I started to catch my flow and get in a rhythm. I began to slip inside and rip Kovalev to the body. He had no answers.

At the end of the seventh, Virg reached for more inspiration—in a clip that actually went viral after the fight. "I believe you closed the gap. We gotta win every single round. . . . This is what greatness is! Robinson got up! Leonard got up! Ali got up! You got up! *Do* it!"

I nodded again. My long-time assistant trainer Don Eames pushed my mouthpiece back in my mouth. I bit down on it and went back to work.

When adversity hits, we show who we really are. Whatever is in you, that's what's going to come out.

Virg kept me engaged the whole fight, to the point where I wasn't thinking about the knee. I discovered that Kovalev's punches were strong but he was physically weak. His physical strength did not match his punching power. I could manhandle him whenever I wanted, and that's exactly what I did. Once I found a weakness, I would exploit that weakness until my opponent made me stop.

I loved inside fighting; it's a beautiful struggle, the most intimate form of combat in a boxing ring. If I could draw a fighter into that kind of fight, I'd have them.

Most fighters, when they are facing big punchers, are taught to stay away from the power and do everything possible to avoid it. Fighters exert a lot of energy and don't gain respect in the process. The old adage that you can't hit what you can't see doesn't always work. The reality is that you *will* get hit—can you take it? At some point, you are going to have to fight so you can get your respect. This is what Virg taught.

I'd watched every single one of Kovalev's fights and I knew he hadn't been trained to fight this way. I had barely seen him throw a body shot. I took him back to North Oakland. I dogged him, and he didn't know how to respond. This kind of fight got Kovalev tired; I felt him physically breaking down. That's the best feeling in the world. I could hear him breathing heavy on the inside; I knew I was weakening him.

The crowd responded to the shots I was landing as I mounted my comeback. Periodically, the voices of the commentators would break through and get my attention.

I waited for Kovalev to go to another gear, but deep down I knew he couldn't. All his bad training habits were now showing up. He was being exposed in his biggest moment on the biggest stage.

When the final bell rang, I knew it was close, but I felt like I had done enough. With boxing you never really know what the judges are thinking or how they have scored the fight. Dino Duva, who worked for Roc Nation, got wind of the decision before Michael Buffer could officially make the announcement. He called Virg over to give him the news. Virg then came over to me to relay what he had heard. "Dre, we won. It was close, but we got it by one round." I couldn't celebrate until the official scorecards were read.

Buffer bellowed into the mic: "Ladies and gentlemen, we go to the judges' scorecards after twelve rounds of action. [All three judges] scored the contest 114–113; to the winner, by unanimous decision, and new unified light heavyweight champion of the world, still undefeated—Andre S.O.G. Ward!"

The first thing I did was jump onto the ropes as I heard an assortment of cheers and boos. I let out all the emotions, pressure, and expectations I had been carrying. When I looked at the crowd, I saw a lot of happy faces. My family and supporters celebrated with me, but I saw lot of disappointment, too, much of it coming from press row.

That night I celebrated with my family as the aches and pains of battle began to surface. The amount of stress you are under and the adrenaline you feel in those moments are truly hard to describe unless you've been in similar situations. As the adrenaline starts to wane, the reality of what you have put your body through begins to speak very loudly.

I woke up the next day and jumped on the treadmill in my suite to loosen my body up. I checked my phone, looked at my social media accounts, and read a few articles to get a feel of what the reaction was from the fight. I read some headlines that said that Kovalev got robbed or Ward got a gift. I wasn't really surprised by what I read, but I *was* disappointed. I was thinking, *Here we go again.* Every significant moment that I've had in my career, there was always a caveat to why I had won. I had become accustomed to this treatment; it came with the territory.

I've never had a problem with anyone feeling like the judges should have said I lost—it was that kind of fight that ebbs and flows. It could have gone either way. I would have no argument if I had lost by a point or two. A fight as close as the one Kovalev and I fought, it's impossible to say that *either* one of us got robbed. A knockdown is polarizing, especially for fans who don't really understand boxing. Of course, Kovalev also had moments after the knockdown, but based on the headlines heading into the fight, I shouldn't have been around for the final bell.

I learned somewhere along the way that people get tired of seeing you win. I haven't lost a fight since I was fourteen years old, but in my mind even a close fight could be considered a loss. It's the same standard that Mayweather was under for his entire boxing career. It's exciting to see a winner taste defeat. That's just human nature. I get that, but I would not apologize for digging deep and winning a close fight. This fight would become my crowning achievement and my favorite fight. I proved I wasn't a front-runner—I showed resilience against a feared champion. It was my badge of honor.

SIXTEEN

REMOVE THE DOUBT

After the first fight with Kovalev, I stayed away from the gym for three months. It was the first time in my life I'd ever done that. Even during the lawsuit, I trained throughout the nearly two-year hiatus. But after the fight with Kovalev and everything that happened in camp, I was mentally and physically exhausted. The knee injury and everything that came with preparing for a big fight had taken a toll on me. I was also dealing with the fallout from the controversial decision. Even though the fight with Kovalev was a great fight and I had taken the fight that no other fighter really wanted, it still seemed that that wasn't good enough. I concluded that there was always going to be something wrong with me, something for them to pick at.

I never spoke publicly about my knee before or after the fight. I'm old school, and that's just how I was raised. For most of the fight, I didn't feel the knee. Adrenaline is a powerful thing. I was fighting for my life; I couldn't afford to worry about the knee. Toward the end of the fight, I could tell it was very swollen. The next day, once the adrenaline had worn off, I had a noticeable limp. The knee had swollen to three times its normal size.

I'm convinced that the sting I felt about the decision was God at work in my life. It was his way of telling me, *Son, it's almost time.* I will always love the sport, but I also know that the sport doesn't always love you back. It will move on to somebody else very quickly. The bitter taste in my mouth was a sign that I needed to seriously think about walking away.

The Kovalev contract had a rematch clause, which meant that if I was going to continue to fight, the rematch with Kovalev was mandatory. For several months after the first fight, I truly believed I would never fight again. I was thirty-three and had been fighting for most of my life. Retirement was a real possibility. In fact, when I was a kid, I always said I would retire at thirty-three. I don't even know where I got that number. That's something that only my family members knew. I never really knew if that was going to be the case, but it was interesting how my life was lining up.

As I stayed away from the gym, I didn't want to talk about boxing. I didn't want to read about boxing. I was good, spending time with my wife and kids, enjoying the life of a family man. But when I started hearing from Prince and Josh, I knew it was time to talk about business and a decision was going to have to be made about my future.

"So we talked to Roc Nation," they told me. "They want to do the rematch. But here's the thing: Roc Nation wants to pay you the same amount as they did for the first fight."

At that moment, the conversation shifted from a casual discussion about business to me letting them know I felt disrespected, not by my team, but by the offer. At that stage in my career, I couldn't afford to take a penny less than what I was worth. My *next* move had to be my *best* move.

I asked them, "Are y'all cool with this?

"No, not necessarily," Josh responded. "We are just relaying the message."

"I'm not fighting for the same amount of money under any circumstances. I'm going on vacation with my family," I said. "Y'all gotta get the money up or there won't be a second fight."

I knew that Josh and Prince were the men for the job and that they would deliver.

Deep down I was still pondering my next move, and I still wasn't sure if I was going to fight again. I began to wonder if the money issue was another sign, telling me that I should no longer fight.

Before my family and I left for vacation, I was in Los Angeles eating at a popular restaurant with my brother Andre Berto. He knows all the best spots to eat in LA. When we walked out of the restaurant, somebody from TMZ was outside, eager to point a camera in my face. He asked me about a potential rematch with Kovalev and if I would be willing to fight him again. I took this as an opportunity to get my message across loud and clear. "I'm not opposed to a rematch, but I don't have to fight anymore. I just want what's fair."

When that hit the airwaves, my team went crazy.

My phone rang the next day. It was Josh and Prince again.

Josh said that Roc Nation wasn't happy with my interview and that this would hurt the negotiations for a rematch. I acknowledged that it might but that I felt strongly about my position.

After I got off the phone, I didn't talk to anybody from my team for about two weeks. We went on our vacation to the Caribbean and had a great time. Our family really needed it. I realized that my family was going through training camp right along with me. The kids were without their dad and my wife was without her husband, shouldering everything on her own. Those moments as a family were essential. We were enjoying the fruits of our labor. My wife and kids deserved that and more.

A few days after I returned from my vacation, I got a call from Prince.

"Dre, I've got good news. We got the money up significantly and I think you will be happy," he said.

I didn't show my hand to Prince on whether I was pleased or not with the Roc Nation offer. At this point I was still negotiating with my team to make sure I wasn't leaving any money on the table.

I told Prince to give me a couple of weeks to think about it. In the meantime, I set up a meeting with my pastor. He had already walked the road I was traveling and had done it successfully. He'd abruptly retired from professional football after six seasons, walking away from the Raiders and millions of dollars while still in his prime at the age of twenty-seven to follow his calling in ministry, preaching the gospel. Deep down, my dream was to leave boxing the exact same way. I wanted to meet with him to see how he felt about me retiring. I assumed he was going to cosign how I was feeling and give me the confirmation I was looking for to walk away. I sat in his office and told him what was on my mind and heart. I conveyed the fact that my fire and love for the sport were gone, that I hadn't walked into a gym for the last three months, and that I wasn't even interested in *talking* about boxing.

He sat there for a second without speaking, then looked at me intently. "Dre, I can see you doing one more," he finally said.

I was shocked. That was not at all what I expected him to say.

"You will be fine if you retire right now," he continued. "God is going to be with you regardless. But I can see you doing one more fight."

After sitting there for a few seconds, I responded, "But I don't have the desire anymore."

"That's okay; the fire will be rekindled when you get back in that gym. Once you get back in your element, the fire will come back." He looked at me closely. "So just pray about it and see what God says."

I left his office feeling deflated and disappointed. I had gone there to get a confirmation of my decision to retire. I didn't get what I wanted, but he gave me what I needed. Anytime I would talk about retirement in the past to either my wife or Virg, they would always have a reason why it wasn't time and an explanation of why I should continue to fight. Initially, this felt like another one of those moments. But the more I thought about it, I felt something shift inside of me and I accepted what my pastor told me. Even though I wasn't going to retire right now, I knew that day wasn't far off. As I drove away, I started crying. I thought about what it would feel like when I ultimately walked away and how much I would miss the sport. I had boxed for over two decades of my life, and as much as I wanted to walk away at times, retirement was not going to be easy. That night, I texted Pastor Napoleon and told him that he might be right—maybe I did have one more in me.

A few weeks later, I accepted the fight with Kovalev. The rematch was on.

I learned more about Kovalev after our first encounter than I did from the twenty rounds that we fought together in the ring. Anytime he was given the opportunity to speak about the fight, he would make many claims and excuses. He showed no accountability and took no responsibility for losing. He blamed everyone but himself.

Kovalev continued to call me various names in the media, saying he was going to slap me when he saw me. He was still unraveling from the loss. When the press tour kicked off, I came ready for anything. This was a multi-city tour. I didn't leave home without my Jordan sneakers. If Kovalev's intent was really to put his hands on me, I wasn't going to be sliding around on stage looking for footing—I was going to be prepared. I wouldn't start anything, but I was ready to finish it.

We finished the tour with no real incidents, but the energy in the room was certainly different than the first media tour, and it was clear that we did not like each other. There was a cloud of doubt around my victory.

For training camp, I made the decision to go back to my roots, my old training regimen. The first day I walked in the gym, Virg said, "We're going to stop him. We're going to knock him out."

"Oh yeah?" I said.

"To the body, we are going to wear him down and stop him with a body attack."

I wasn't going to argue with him. I shook my head and said, "Okay."

We needed to make sure my knee was right. During my three-month break, I was able to rest the knee and allow it to heal. I went back to my strength coach, Aaron Thigpen. I'd worked with Aaron for years and he knew exactly how to train my mind and my body. The first order of business was to strengthen my legs through functional training that would translate to the boxing ring. We had to rebuild my body from the ground up. Aaron said that we needed to strengthen my ankles and start to build from there. If your ankles are out of alignment, it will affect your knees.

As we trained, my knee grew stronger, and my legs had bounce again. Unlike the first fight, it was imperative to get off to a fast start to establish what kind of pace we were going to fight at. We knew Kovalev had a conditioning problem, and that was confirmed in our first encounter. I wore him down; he was weakened by my body attack and physical strength. He could not keep me off him. Kovalev had become accustomed to his opponents fearing him and allowing him to fight at a comfortable pace. We wanted to finish what we started, round thirteen. This time I had to be better.

I carried one big secret into training camp: I knew this would be my last fight. This decision gave me the strength to endure another camp and take the rematch. I didn't need to prove anything to myself or anyone else. Acknowledging that this was my last dance afforded me comfort on one hand and urgency on the other. If this was going to be my last fight, we had to get it right. I work best when the margin for error is slim and my back is against the wall. Virg knew nothing about my decision. Only my wife, my publicist, and a few of my brothers who I could count on one hand knew. I didn't want Virg to treat me any differently during camp. There are days that I feel bad that I did not give Virg a heads-up. At that time, I felt it was best to keep silent.

I left home seven weeks before the fight and moved into my training condo that I rented about twenty minutes from the gym. This turned out to be the best camp of my career. It's almost like God extended me some extra grace because this would be my last fight. I felt like the wind was at my back. Training was hard but I enjoyed it; I was happy and having fun again. I was doing things in camp I hadn't done in years. Anyone who came in would notice the form I was in and they would comment that the adjustments we'd made were evident. That extra fire in me showed up throughout camp. I would usually be up at 5:00 a.m. to do my cardio, out the door by 5:30, but this camp, I would wake up at 3:30 a.m. to wake up my assistant trainer Edward "Jack" Jackson. Jack has been an integral part of my team since the beginning of my professional career. I'm not sure I could have reached the heights I reached without him. He wore many hats in camp—being my security and my strength-and-conditioning coach. He even washed and folded my laundry and was always there to encourage me, especially on bad days in the gym. Jack was the only one who lived with me in training camp. Most days, we had a great time, but Jack also had to deal with me on my worst days and he always did it gracefully.

"Jack, you up?"

"I am now—what's up?"

"Hey bro, let's get it. I'm ready to go," I would say.

"But it's 3:30," he'd respond.

"I know, but I'm up, time to work!"

Often, I'd finish my workouts as the sun was coming up. I knew Kovalev was still asleep; I knew I was more focused and that I was outworking him. I had new life with my training: my perspective was different, my energy was different—*I* was different. Kovalev had big problems on the horizon; he just didn't know it yet.

Even the media workout felt different. Media workouts for big fights typically happen three to four weeks before the fight. This gives the media one last opportunity to analyze both fighters physically and mentally. On this occasion, I blew through my media workout and, most importantly, I enjoyed everything about it. I savored the moment, knowing it would be my last.

Team Kovalev continued to yap away about one thing or another, looking for sympathy after losing the first fight. Kathy Duva is a seasoned promoter who had been in the boxing trenches long before I'd set foot in a professional boxing ring. She was trying to make noise about her fighter losing the first fight to gain benevolence from the Nevada Athletic Commission, fight fans, and the judges who would be scoring our rematch. Crafty, but we knew what was going on. I had to trust the process and stay focused. The mission was to stop Sergey Kovalev. I knew if I allowed our rematch to be close, it was more than likely going to swing his way. I also didn't want a trilogy. If I lost the second fight, it would immediately justify the notion that Kovalev had really won the first fight. I'd have been on the hook for another training camp, more pain, and time away from the family.

Before the second fight was officially signed, Kovalev's trainer

John David Jackson quietly reached out to Josh to air out grievances he had against Kovalev. They were not getting along, and Jackson was growing discontent. He complained that Kovalev did not listen to him in the first training camp or in the first fight, nor did Jackson feel respected as a trainer. This was not new; this dynamic between the two of them had been going on for quite some time. Jackson was unhappy because he would give Kovalev instructions in the gym and in the fight but he felt the Russian translator was giving Kovalev different instructions. Jackson would instruct Kovalev to do specific drills and he would refuse. He would tell him to spar a certain amount of rounds but he would want to do his own thing. It was no secret that Kovalev didn't always live the lifestyle of a fighter outside the gym, and that was confirmed in our first fight. Jackson was concerned that he was on the verge of getting fired as Team Kovalev was internally blaming him for the loss.

He was a former champion who was respected and had dog in him and didn't appreciate how he was being handled. This compelled him to pick up the phone and reach out to Josh. As I've mentioned, Josh is not just my lawyer but also a good friend.

The idea was floated for Jackson, who might be getting fired, to join Team Ward. Kovalev losing to me further created ruptures in their relationship. If Kovalev had won, like many expected, I'm sure most of their problems would have remained beneath the surface. Winning covers a multitude of sins.

When I first got wind of the possibility, my initial thought was, *This might be interesting. This would be the ultimate checkmate.* Prince also thought the idea was interesting and entertained it but was unsure if it was the right move to make.

The idea of Jackson coming to my team was floated to Virg, and he had mixed feelings. Virg was the ultimate prefight strategist, looking to cause disruption and chaos in the opposite camp as much as he could. But joining forces with someone like Jackson after all that had been said and done left Virg unsure about how to proceed. Internal talks continued for another week or two with there being a negotiation between Prince, Josh, and Jackson in the interim. I stayed away and kept my distance. I ultimately picked up the phone and told Virg that we didn't need Jackson, that even if we had him sign a non-disclosure agreement, we couldn't trust him to not leak information to Team Kovalev.

"And when we beat him again, Virg, I don't want any credit taken away from you," I told him. "I can read the headlines now: 'Team Ward Needed Help from Kovalev Trainer to Get the Job Done in Rematch.'"

We knew how the media played. Those narratives would be too juicy to pass up. I couldn't give them that kind of ammunition. I respected my godfather too much. He deserved to get all the credit that was coming his way if the second fight turned out the way we believed it would.

Virg quickly agreed. "You're right, baby, we don't need him."

Deep down, I think Virg felt empathy for John David Jackson for being treated so poorly. Virg knew the plight of many of the African American trainers in the game. They don't always get the credit they deserve nor receive their just due when annual awards come around. Many will refute this notion, but it's true. There are too many case studies that confirm this point.

My feelings about not bringing Jackson to our camp were confirmed by how the financial negotiations played out. The man asked for a king's ransom to join Team Ward. He didn't realize that he didn't have any leverage. He was a man without a home, unsure if he would return to Team Kovalev or if he was welcome on my team. Shortly after Jackson got the word that we were no longer entertaining the idea, he and Kovalev made up and he remained on his team for the second fight. But the damage was done.

Josh and Prince strongly believed that Jackson would attempt to get ahead of the story and say that my team reached out to him first, which was blatantly untrue. We kept receipts.

The upcoming media workout, midway through our training camps, was the perfect time to discuss what had happened and play our ace card. I instructed Josh and Prince to make sure my media workout happened first, the day before Kovalev's. It was important for me to speak first and get the truth out. I also knew that this would be a major blow to Kovalev's camp once I shot this missile.

With the cameras pointed at me, I proceeded to bring down the events that took place. I told the truth and nothing but the truth. The media seemed shocked and confused about these revelations. The next day we watched the footage as Jackson did a terrible job of trying to explain the situation while Kovalev looked on, seemingly confused and angry. The missile had landed. If Kovalev had fired Jackson just three weeks before the fight, it would confirm all the rumors about him and his trainer. It was easier to keep the team intact, at least superficially, and just deny the facts.

We finished training camp strong. The mission and message never changed: we were going to stop Kovalev, knock him out. Many turned their up nose in disbelief. "Yeah, right—you barely won the first one. How are you going to stop him?" I couldn't argue with those sentiments; I simply had to show them.

The end of my career was near, and I knew it, but I kept my feelings close to the vest. The other reason I didn't tell Virg about my retirement plans was that I wanted the option to change my mind if I felt different after the fight. This would be unknown territory, and I needed to give myself some space and grace in case I changed my mind.

Unlike the week before the first fight, this time I was at peace going into my final week of preparations. Don't get me wrong, the pressure was palpable and very real. When a big fight descends on Las Vegas, you can feel the presence and energy of the fans.

Doubt, fear, and the glaring question of *Have I done enough?* will always show up. How you fight *those* battles will determine how you perform on fight night. "For as he thinks in his heart, so is he" (Proverbs 23:7). If you believe the lie that you don't belong, you won't belong. If you believe the stage is too big, it will be.

I was as fit and ready both mentally and physically as I had ever been.

I was ready for war.

SEVENTEEN

CENTER STAGE

During fight week, the weigh-in was my favorite thing to do. It was the last stop before we could finally hydrate and eat what we wanted. Sometimes, I'd have to cut an extreme amount of weight during the last three weeks before a fight, on an already lean body. There were so many times I would need to lose eight to ten pounds, and I would look at my physique and wonder how in the world was I going to lose it. Virg would grab some skin on my stomach and say, "Oh yeah—you've got room to lose it right here." I'd give him the side eye and think, *Easy for you to say—you're not the one losing the weight.*

I'm not an internet dude. I don't talk loud on social media. I like being face-to-face. I want to look into my opponents' eyes and feel where they are coming from. The eyes never lie. The weigh-ins afforded me this opportunity. These moments don't mean everything, but they certainly mean something. You can feel if someone is afraid or showing too much respect. All of these are indicators for both fighters. I tried to look right through Kovalev as we locked eyes. I never wanted to be the first one to turn away and break the stare. During our face-off, I could have stayed on that MGM Grand stage all night; I wasn't going to budge. The crowd was hollering, going crazy. Kovalev broke his stare first. This set the tone for the following night.

It got lonely at the house I was renting in Las Vegas. My family and friends were out having a good time while I was back at the house trying to get my mind ready for battle. Those were sobering moments with just me and God. All the training and sacrifices were for this moment.

That night, I slept good. As I opened my eyes the next morning, I smiled. It was fight day. The hours before the fight can feel excruciatingly long. My chef came and dropped off my food for the entire day: my breakfast, lunch, and my prefight meal. After eating and hydrating after the weigh-in, I had put on about thirteen pounds overnight. I looked a lot bigger for this fight than I did for our first.

The fight stayed on my mind throughout the day—so much so that I would catch myself flinching from imaginary punches while I slept and when I was awake. I couldn't get the Russian out of my mind. I wouldn't have complete peace until I finished the job and closed this chapter for good.

The house I was staying in was about ten minutes from the Las Vegas Strip. I could have stayed in my Skyloft at Mandalay Bay, where the fight was taking place, but I gave that space to my wife and kids. I didn't want to be in the hotel, surrounded by all the prefight commotion, needing to go through the back corridors in order to move around. But I was excited about fighting at Mandalay Bay Events Center—I had dreamed of this day ever since I saw Floyd Mayweather fight there when I was still an amateur.

When I got to the arena, I jumped out of my Sprinter van with my crew. I felt the kind of nerves that only come from being on the big stage. This was the happiest I had ever been going into a fight. The HBO producer informed me that I would be walking to the ring between 8:45 and 9:15 p.m. This left me with about two and a half hours to get ready.

I took a seat on the black leather couch in my locker room next to Virg. It wasn't lost on me that this might be the last time he and I would take this ride together. Virg would periodically lean in and whisper, "It's your time; be great tonight." I loved these moments; Virg always knew the right things to tell me before battle. I would always put my boxing shoes on first, get my hands wrapped, then it was time to get dressed. I slipped on my protector cup, then my boxing trunks, and slowly started to stretch and warm up. My team had to constantly manage the door to my locker room, especially in Vegas. People are constantly trying to come in for various reasons—celebrities, older fighters, and people who want to wish you luck. I knew that I needed to manage my energy. My brother Damian Lillard from the Portland Trail Blazers came in; Marshawn Lynch and a few others were there. I consider these people family, and when family is around, I gain energy from their presence. The boxing commissioners were constantly hovering to make sure no one was breaking the rules. HBO cameramen were in and out, grabbing a few minutes of footage for the viewing audience at home and in the arena, then they would zip out of the room.

In the midst of this chaos, I stayed within myself and allowed the craziness to happen around me. My body was in the room, but my mind was already fighting Kovalev. The walk to the ring and the fight itself would be more chaotic than this locker room.

Virg grabbed his mitts and we started to do our thing—*pop pop pop*. As I moved and felt my rhythm, I took some deep breaths. The moment was upon us; it was time. The HBO producer came barreling through the door. "It's time for you to walk!"

We stopped warming up, gathered in a circle, and began to pray. I didn't ever lead the prayer, but Virg or someone from my team would step up. This was the quiet before the storm. "Amen," I heard. The HBO cameras were bright—the world was watching.

As I stepped through the legendary hallway of Mandalay Bay, I took in everything—the brownish brick walls, the hard concrete floor. I thought about all the great fighters who had made the same walk. As we moved farther away from the locker room, I could feel the anticipation growing. Standing in the tunnel, I could barely see the ring. All I could hear were rabid fans calling for blood. As we got closer to the ring, I saw Russian and American flags.

I ascended to the top of the steps, saluted the crowd, and made eye contact with my wife and kids and blew them a kiss. Then I ducked underneath the ropes and I turned into a different man, one who was willing to do whatever it took to leave with my belts and dignity.

I bounced around the ring, touching every corner and letting it be known: *This is* my *ring!* I looked at Kovalev to see if he would make eye contact. He did. I went to my corner and knelt and prayed.

I paced back and forth, looking at the crowd, nodding at the people, throwing combinations, while I stayed loose. Everything felt perfect.

In the first fight, I had been stationary the first two rounds. Kovalev took full advantage. This time would be much different. I never stayed still, even if it was just subtle movements and little feints. I always wanted to look like I was doing something, even if I really wasn't. I needed to keep the puncher off-balance. Each round it got worse and worse for Kovalev. My power was on point that night. I was hitting him with big shots. I started to touch him even more, especially to the body, just like we had planned. Kovalev didn't like the body shots from the first fight so the adjustment he made was to pull his protective cup and trunks way above his navel to try to protect himself. In the prefight instructions, referee Tony Weeks had looked at Kovalev's beltline and told him his beltline was a little high, meaning that a punch there would be a legal blow.

Kovalev was frustrated because nothing was working for him. Anytime Kovalev landed, I would eat the shot and hit him right back in the face. I manhandled him and beat him up on the inside and confused him on the outside. At the start of every round, I made sure to get in a big shot, to send a message: *I'm here. I'm not going nowhere.* By the seventh, I could tell Kovalev was fading. I hit him with a little baby body shot to the beltline and he looked to the referee for help. Instead of attacking him, I took a step back, but it was clear to me he was looking for a way out. *Dude, your name is Krusher—why are you looking for help?*

In the corner, Virg agreed. "He's ready to go," Virg told me. "That's why he's complaining. We know what that means."

On the HBO telecast, Roy Jones Jr. was seeing it, too. He said Kovalev needed to stop reacting to the borderline shots because it was giving me confidence. Roy was right about that. When I came out for the eighth round, I was thinking that it was time to step it up and stop him. Kovalev backed me to the ropes as I slightly turned my body and started to walk toward him. I threw a jab just to blind him and followed with a big right hand that hurt him. *Boom!* Kovalev wobbled. He was badly hurt. I walked him down and went back to the body. I started punishing him to the body and he did everything in his power to hold on. I was beating him around the ring as the crowd was in a frenzy, but all I was focused on was getting Kovalev out of there. I backed him in my corner along the ropes and tried to finish him off.

Kovalev was bent over in a fetal position, a sign that he had conceded. I kept ripping to the body as Weeks stepped in and waved off the fight, signaling the end and erasing all doubt. I was a little surprised Weeks stopped it. I thought he was going to let me jump back on him. *I'll take it, though.* I walked around the ring with my hand raised in victory, climbed on the ropes, and let out a yell. This was for the ones who believed in me and never stopped supporting me. This was for us.

I typically didn't bring my wife into the ring with me after my fights. She is my queen, and my level of respect for her is hard to explain. I only wanted to go to war for my family, get my check, and hand it to my wife. I never wanted her to step foot in the ring; it was marred with dirt, both literally and figuratively. I felt this was no place for my queen to be—until that night. If this would be the last one, I wanted her to join me and experience this moment.

Before I exited the ring, HBO's Max Kellerman proclaimed, "I think you are the top pound-for-pound fighter in the world tonight."

That night, we celebrated with the ones we loved: family and close friends. I had a few bumps and bruises, a small price to pay to cement my legacy and leave Vegas a winner. There is a peculiar enjoyment that comes with the pain that reminds you that you've been to battle and you made it out.

Shortly after the fight, I started hearing rumblings of another controversy. This time, I was being accused of hitting Kovalev low at the end of the fight. I wasn't going to let these excuses steal my joy. *Not tonight.* I guess Kovalev and his people forgot about the right hand that came close to knocking him out shortly before the fight was stopped.

We stayed in Vegas for two days. I was fighting the heaviness that sometimes visits athletes and entertainers after a big moment. I had just been in a life-or-death situation, and my adrenaline was at an all-time high. Suddenly, it was all over. The adrenaline begins to rapidly dissipate along with your mood, and you can quickly feel depressed. For the last seven weeks, I'd only wanted to win and be reunited with my family. *I got what I wanted and now I'm feeling this way?* I learned to fight this through prayer and by allowing myself forty-eight to seventy-two hours to "come down"—to decompress and not do much until I felt like myself again.

We boarded a private jet and returned to Oakland two days after the fight. I couldn't help but reflect in that moment about some of the places I'd had to fight early in my career. There I was, flying to and from my fight on a private jet with all my senses intact and depositing a very big check into my bank account. Mission accomplished. I had done everything I set out to do in the sport of boxing.

EIGHTEEN

IS THIS THE END?

Although I had strong feelings about retirement before the second Kovalev fight, my mind was not fully made up yet. It wasn't long before I was in a position again where I had to make some decisions about my future. I had a new Jordan deal on the table awaiting my signature—three times what my previous deal was. HBO had quickly approached me with a new deal as well. They were going to give me a tune-up fight in Oakland after my last fight, sort of like a victory lap. It was for a lot of money. HBO was also willing to renew my broadcasting deal. I was the best fighter in the world, and the deals that I had on the table reflected that. Everything I ever wanted in the sport was right in front me.

I was scheduled to commentate for the championship rematch between super flyweights Srisaket Sor Rungvisai of Thailand and Román "Chocolatito" González of Nicaragua, slated for September 9, 2017. HBO wanted to announce my new deals that were on the table the day before the fight took place, but before I could get on the plane, something shifted. I had been training with my strength-and-conditioning coach, Aaron, and going to the boxing gym, slowly preparing my body to fight again. But I woke up the day before I was scheduled to leave for the fight, got dressed, and just laid on the floor. I felt a heaviness and was fighting back tears.

"What's wrong?" my wife asked as she entered the room. She sounded concerned.

"I don't know if I want to keep boxing," I said.

She had heard this before. I'd told her several times throughout the years that I wanted to retire. She would always encourage me but ultimately tell me that it wasn't time.

"Really? You feel like that?" she asked.

"I don't know. It's not feeling right to me. I canceled all my training yesterday and today," I told her.

"Well, let me get the kids together," she responded. "We'll talk a little bit later." And she was gone. The whole day, I was mulling over my decision, thinking and praying. I was trying to understand what was happening to me and why I was feeling this way.

One of the deacons at my church, Robert Jenkins, a former offensive lineman for the Los Angeles Rams and the Los Angeles and Oakland Raiders, would often talk to me about retirement. I would always pick his brain and ask a lot of questions because I knew my day would come. I studied my pastor's exit from professional sports, as well as the exits of Jim Brown, Barry Sanders, and Marshawn Lynch. Deacon Rob would always tell me, "One day you're going to wake up and not want to do it anymore."

That never made sense when I was an active fighter, yet that day I knew exactly what he was talking about.

Me and Tiffiney finally had a chance later that night to follow up on our earlier conversation. After we talked for a few minutes, she looked at me and said, "Babe, I think the decision is already made."

I was shocked. I don't really know what I was expecting her to say in that moment, but it wasn't that. She could see the shock on my face.

"Dre, I've never heard you talk like this before," she explained. She was referencing me telling her that I wasn't trying to take any more punches and I wasn't trying to dish out any more punches.

"When I hear you say that, I know that this is it," she said.

I understood what she was saying, though I do believe if I willed my way through, I would have gotten my mind together and figured it out like I had done many times before. But I had to acknowledge that this was different. When we finished talking, I felt a huge sense of relief. I immediately went downstairs and called Josh. Over the previous years Josh would always hint that he wanted me to retire, especially when I was going through my right-knee issues. When he saw how bad my knee was before the first Kovalev fight, he said, "Bro, you've got to stop."

"Nah, man, I'm good. It's not time yet," I told him.

When I went downstairs and told him that I had decided to retire, his response was, "Alright, that's it. I'm about to call—"

"Whoa, whoa, whoa! I'm just telling you what just happened. Calm down! I'm not saying I'm doing this. I'm saying I think this is what I'm about to do."

"Bro, listen to me," he said. "This is what you need to do. If your wife is on board and you feel like this, you need to do it."

"Yeah, but I don't know. Like, bro, the money . . ."

"I thought you said you would never box just for money, that that wouldn't be enough of a reason."

I did say that, didn't I? I thought. It was a checkmate.

"Okay, let me think this through. Let me sleep on it. I just wanted to give you a heads-up."

The next morning, I felt like pulling the plug on the retirement talk and doing what was easiest: keep fighting. Retirement would shake up our world, and I would be leaving a lot of money on the table. But later that day, I called Josh to confirm that what I said the night before wasn't an aberration, it was real. "I'm done. What do we need to do now?"

"Sit tight. Let me call HBO and tell them to hold off on announcing the new deal. Dre, you need to call Prince."

I knew Prince was next on my list to call. He was expecting us to sign this new deal within a few days. Part of the reason I waited to tell Prince was because I didn't want to disappoint him. He played his cards the way I knew he would—close to the vest.

"So you think you're done, huh?" he asked.

"I do. I'm done, J."

"You sure about that?" he said.

"Yeah, I think I'm sure." I listed all the reasons.

He said, "We are going to support you." I could tell I had just knocked the wind out of him. That hurt me. I felt like I was doing the right thing, but it was still extremely difficult because I knew I would hurt some people in the process. The next person I needed to speak to was Virg, but I couldn't bring myself to tell him just yet.

I first had to begin to "undo" all of my new deals that had been agreed to in principle, but not yet signed. Self-preservation tried to take over. Maybe I should do just one more fight, lock in the new Jordan deal, and get one more check from HBO. I didn't want to mislead anyone, and for a moment the idea seemed genius, but things quickly shifted. God began to deal with me, and my conscience was troubled by the idea of signing a new deal when I had no intentions of honoring the contract. All money isn't good money, and you have to know when to leave the bad money on the table.

I also called Larry Miller, my good friend and the former president of the Jordan Brand. "Larry, I can't take this deal," I told him. "I'm gonna retire."

Larry was shocked but respected the way I was going about things. He assured me that we would still do some sort of deal with me as a brand ambassador. "Dre, you are a Jordan athlete for life."

I told HBO that I needed to wait on the announcement for my next fight. I got a lot of questions that weekend, but somehow I was able to hold on to the enormous secret the whole time. No one at HBO suspected that my delay in announcing our new deal had anything to do with retirement. Josh told them I had a few personal things I needed to sort out. Being at the fights that weekend and carrying the weight of my impending retirement was difficult. If there was any time to change my mind and abort the plan, it was then. I asked myself, *You going to be okay walking away? Once you walk away, that's it.* But my answer remained the same: *I'm ready.*

I got through that weekend without incident and my mind was still made up. But how was I going to announce it? I thought about one of those impromptu press conferences where the media doesn't really know why they are there. That wasn't it. Maybe I should have my publicist write something and release it to the world and be done that way? That wasn't it either. I wouldn't be able to capture my thoughts in a meaningful way; my letter to boxing would be too long. Then it hit me.

I chose to do a strong visual retirement that my close friend Diaunte and I produced and directed. The Jordan Brand wanted to partner with me and make the announcement a joint venture. I felt that would only make the announcement stronger. Each of my three sons were featured in the video portraying the different stages of my career—amateur boxing, the Olympics, and the pro ranks. We shot the video at my boxing gym. I made sure no one was there, not even Virg. We shot everything we needed in one day.

As we edited the video, I was still surveying my heart. Was I ready for this? I was. Or at least as ready as I was going to be.

Ironically, two of my proudest moments in boxing were negotiating and keeping my Roc Nation deal quiet before it was announced and retiring at the peak of my career and successfully keeping it a secret.

On September 21, 2017, only three months after my career-defining victory over Sergey Kovalev, I walked away from the sport for good. Boxing and I officially parted ways on that day. We gathered in my living room, and I was feeling the all-too-familiar nerves and angst I'd always felt before a big fight. My film crew was there along with my family. I hit send on my retirement video on Instagram and Twitter, revealed my big secret, and made my retirement official. As we watched the world's reaction in real time, I didn't know how to feel. The prevailing emotion was pride. I was proud of myself and what I'd been able to accomplish in a sport like boxing. Many great men have not made it out whole. By the grace of God, I would be an exception. The video concluded with just two words: *Mission Accomplished.* My phone was blowing up with interview requests; everybody wanted to talk to me. But I chose to just talk to Stephen A. Smith and Max Kellerman on *First Take* on ESPN. Everything felt surreal. I concluded my interview and spent most of the day driving around trying to understand what I had just done. I picked my kids up from school later that day. "Dad, everyone was shocked. They can't believe you walked away," my son Malachi said.

Tiffiney has always been a rock. But it took me a year or so into retirement before I realized that it meant *she* was retiring too. I was so focused on myself that I would forget to ask her, "How are you dealing with this?" Some wives would be relieved their husbands didn't have to go to training camp anymore and that they didn't have to watch them fight. But Tiffiney never worried about me in the ring. She never felt like I was going to get hurt when I stepped in there. Her thinking was, "You are going to be fine because God's got you." And she felt I was the best. But when I stepped away, we both had to figure out how to adjust to our new lives.

On a good day, I know I did the right thing and left at the right time. On my worst day, I'm asking myself, *What were you thinking?* I tease Tiffiney too: "Girl, why didn't you talk me out of retiring? We could have made sixty million by now." She fires back with, "Do you remember how you were looking and sounding at that time?"

She has a point.

I finally spoke to Virg the night before I retired. I don't really know why I waited until the last minute. I'm not saying it was right, but that is just the way I felt compelled to handle it.

"Virg, I need to talk to you," I told him over the phone.

"What's up, baby?"

"Man, I think I'm done."

There was silence on the other end. Finally, Virg said, "Oh yeah?"

"I feel like I got the green light from God to walk away." His response surprised me.

"I'm not sad at all," he said. Similar to how it had been with Prince, I knew this was not the full truth. Even if he wasn't sad at that moment, I knew it would hit him later on. "We did it the right way," he continued. "This is the way we always talked about leaving the sport. They never got the last laugh, did they?"

"No, they didn't."

"They never saw you with a bloody nose. Knocked out. We did it the right way. I'm happy for you. And I'm proud."

Even as Virg spoke, I realized that retiring was such an Andre

Ward thing to do—just when the world was giving me my due and my marketing ability and power in the sport were at an all-time high, I handed it back and walked the other way. I had given God a return on his investment; I had maxed out on the talent and ability that he had given me. He kept me safe in this brutal sport, and I am so grateful. I never cheated the sport. I did not cheat my family. I dedicated my life to my preparation so I could always put my family in the best position to win. I gave the sport all my effort, but not all of myself. My family deserved to have something left of me when I finally walked away.

"I appreciate you, Virg, more than you know. Thank you for everything," I said. "I just feel like this is God, Virg, and I have to be obedient."

"Do what God is telling you to do, son. And one more thing . . . don't ever come back."

I promised him that I wouldn't, and I have kept my word. Every day that I stay retired is another day that I beat the sport, and this is a fight that I intend to win.

NINETEEN

FIRST-BALLOT HALL OF FAMER

I knew that I had earned the right to be a first-ballot Hall of Famer, but I wasn't confident that the writers and historians who cast the ballots felt the same way. When I won the Super Six, I felt I had done enough to make it in. After beating Chad Dawson and then Sergey Kovalev twice, I believed there was no way it could be taken from me. But I started to obsess over it.

"Dre, you know you have done enough to be a first-ballot Hall of Famer," Tiffiney told me. "Just leave it in God's hands and let him do the rest."

I did just that, and the call finally came. "We are calling to tell you that your name and legacy will be enshrined in the International Boxing Hall of Fame forever," Hall of Fame director Ed Brophy said.

As we spoke, I felt overwhelmed with emotion. The tears started falling. When Brophy was done speaking, I thanked him for the incredible honor. "I can finally rest now," I said.

I had ascended to the highest height, and nobody could take that away from me. Everything we had worked for was about this moment. It was now signed, sealed, and delivered; I felt an enormous sense of relief. I was pleased that my son Malachi was there with me to see that moment unfold in real time, to witness my tears.

As my family and I arrived in Canastota, New York, home of the International Boxing Hall of Fame, I felt the weight of the moment and glory of the legends who were enshrined there. I couldn't help but reflect on my journey that had gotten me there.

My call from Canastota came in 2020, in the middle of the pandemic. I was in the class of 2021, but the induction ceremonies for the 2020 and 2021 classes were postponed. I wasn't happy about the delays, but it turned out to be a blessing. This led to a "trilogy" induction ceremony of three classes, something that had never been done before. I would be inducted at the same time as my big three: Bernard Hopkins (class of 2020), Floyd Mayweather (class of 2021), and Roy Jones Jr. (class of 2022). There was a host of other greats who were inducted that weekend that I had grown up watching, including Ann Wolfe, Laila Ali, James Toney, and many more. I felt like that young kid again who fell in love with boxing at ten years old.

I had to remind myself that I deserved to be here, shoulder to shoulder with these great champions. When I first arrived, my anxiety was on ten. I had to challenge myself to do something that I don't do very well—celebrate my wins and stay in the moment. My wife and Julie Goldsticker, my publicist, were also reminding me to enjoy myself.

One of the highlights of that weekend for me was speaking to Roy Jones Jr. and Bernard Hopkins. Even though I spent time with Roy over the years, and he was even my co-promoter early in my career, I'd never really spent the kind of time with him that I wanted to. I blame myself for that. Roy had always told me, "I'm here; reach out for whatever you need."

I believed him, but I never followed through and took him up on the offer. He told me that when he got my text inviting him to sit down in Canastota, he thought, *I don't know what Andre is texting me about, but I'll be there.* This was a man I tried to model myself after when I was coming up. To hear him say that was powerful for me. When we were done speaking, Roy stood up and said, "This was long overdue."

He was right; it was.

After my conversation with Roy, I ran into Bernard Hopkins. It was that kind of weekend. As I approached him, I saw he was eating. He stood up to greet me, just as intense as ever. Although Bernard is retired and has been for some time, he still wears that North Philly scowl as if he were still fighting. I know that Bernard is very particular about his diet and the foods he eats, so I decided to mess with him.

"You eating that pasta?" I said.

"No, no, no. Who put that pasta there?" Bernard said, looking around the table. He spotted salmon and a salad and said, "That's my plate right there!"

"I see you're not slippin', Hop, you're still on your game," I said jokingly.

Bernard told me he was still only three pounds over his fighting weight. He then congratulated me on my induction. It was a quintessential Bernard Hopkins moment.

It was also special to be able to share the weekend with my mother. Her presence was the greatest gift she could have given me. She overcame a great deal, she survived, and she was there to see her son get inducted into the Hall of Fame. She was having the time of her life.

As I moved through the weekend, I couldn't help but think about my father—he would be so proud of his baby boy.

When you walk into that modest Hall of Fame building in Canastota, you will find my plaque on the wall of Hall of Fame greats. I am literally surrounded by my boxing heroes: Bernard Hopkins is above me, Floyd Mayweather is to the left of me, and Roy Jones Jr. is diagonally to my left, underneath Floyd. This is not a coincidence; this is the way it was supposed to be.

My life has been a culmination of the peaks and valleys that come with life. Some of my trials and tribulations came from my own doing with no one else to blame. Everything else I did not ask for. My struggles taught me invaluable lessons that serve me to this day. I feel like I've been fighting my whole life as if this was a calling. I was a good kid growing up who had a loving family that was fractured. The fractures my parents wore soon became my own. I used this as an excuse to become prideful, and I rebelled. Pride comes before destruction. Hard days were ahead for me. I soon forsook all that I knew. Isolation, drugs, and alcohol became all too familiar. My father's sudden death sent shockwaves through my world. In this place, the devil had a field day. I forgot who I was and who God had called me to be. I completely lost myself.

I was called to lead and to allow myself to be led by the right ones. I was called to be different. I just couldn't see it at the time. It took rock bottom before I was humble enough to look up and cry out for help. It wasn't God's fault my father died; it was a part of life. Can I accept good from God but not accept adversity? It took many years before I could answer that question. For me, Jesus was always a prayer away, and when I called, he answered. He met me where I was. God was merciful to me and didn't allow me to receive the true penalty of what was owed. After my conversion, all I wanted to do was honor God and the ones who went before me: my mom and dad. The best way I could do that would be to take all that they had given me—the good and the bad—and be better. I will honor them both until the day I die.

Boxing has been the metaphor for my life: triumphs and successes followed by intervals of trials and tests. I've faced opposition and giants that were bigger than me, but none were bigger than the God I served. This is a truth I've grown into over the years. I needed to come to the end of myself and lean into him. In doing this, I felt peace and the grace that I needed to continue on.

Neither my mother nor my father are defined by their struggles in my eyes. It's only made me love and respect them all the more. I'm not saying I haven't been affected by their indiscretions and shortcomings, because I most certainly have. I was affected in a profound way. Now I have healed, and so have they. My father was not an addict when he died; he died a healed man. My mother is clean and sober and has been for many years. She's not only in my life, but she is a great example for her grandbabies, and God has allowed her to redeem the time. Anything she missed in my life, she has been that for my children and more. I am so grateful. As a young boy I used to pray every night before I went to bed for God to save my mom and get her off the streets of San Francisco. He has done that and more.

My story is not a sad one but one of redemption. It's not how you start but how you finish. Anyone can change, and everyone is redeemable.

EPILOGUE

It's been several years since my last fight, and I still have to be intentional about my retirement. I've realized that the pull to fight again and to do something that I've done for most of my life is always going to be there. But just because I can still do it doesn't mean I should.

The allure of the bright lights, the need to compete, and the multimillion-dollar paydays make it extremely hard for any athlete to peacefully transition into the next phase of their life. I've seen professional athletes try to replace the high they feel when they're competing with drugs, alcohol, or other harmful behaviors during retirement. I've learned that the key is to retire out of one thing and into something else. My drive, focus, and need to overcome challenges had to shift from boxing to other things. You remain who you are, but the mission changes.

Faith, family, business, and commentating keep me busy, engaged, and full of life. I was cultivating these areas while my boxing career was ongoing. Though I missed time with my kids because of training,

I was still a very present husband and father. I didn't want to retire, come home, and have my wife and kids not really know me.

I've been commentating for over a decade now. I heard many times that I couldn't be an active fighter and commentate at the same time, but that was foolish to me. I saw Roy Jones Jr. and other fighters do it for years, and if they could do it, I could do it too.

My faith in God has been my foundation that allowed me to build my life and career as it now stands. I've been in ministry and served in my local church over the last twenty years. I believe my true calling is to preach the gospel of Jesus Christ.

For me, boxing was a teacher and a training ground to help prepare me for this current season of my life. I've always been blessed to have great people speak into my life; between my father, Virg, and my pastor, the message has always been the same: boxing was what I did; it's not who I am.

ACKNOWLEDGMENTS

I want to thank my beautiful wife, Tiffiney, for being my encouragement, counselor, and editor throughout this process. If you were not here, this book would not get done.

To my five beautiful children for allowing Dad to get lost for hours on end to make this book what it is. Thank you for your tireless support.

To Julie, my publicist/assistant, for countless hours of writing and editing. Your insight, patience, and encouragement have been a difference maker.

I want to thank my friend Devon Franklin for his continued support and encouragement, and for connecting me with Nena Oshman along with the best literary agent in the world, Jan Miller.

To Minister Kathryn for your insight and your confirming voice that this book needed to be written.

To my brother Shaka Singore, one of the most gifted writers I know. Thank you for always picking up the phone and for encouraging me not to shrink back, but to press in and tell the world this story.

ABOUT THE AUTHORS

ANDRE WARD is married to his high school sweetheart, Tiffiney. Together with their five children, they live in the San Francisco Bay Area. He is a retired world champion and Hall of Fame boxer, as well as a licensed minister and youth pastor at his church, The Well Christian Community in Livermore, California. Andre enjoys spending his time with his family, serving his community, and speaking at churches, corporations, and colleges. Andre and his wife view writing as a passion and a ministry and they look forward to writing more books in the near future.

Over the course of his thirty-six-year career, NICK CHILES has distinguished himself as a bestselling author and an award-winning journalist. He is the author or coauthor of twenty-one books, including four *New York Times* bestsellers.